SPAIN

SPAIN

A Personal Anthology

compiled by

THOMAS HINDE

NEWNES : LONDON

First Published 1963

Made and printed in Great Britain by
The Garden City Press Limited, Letchworth, Hertfordshire
for George Newnes Limited, Tower House
Southampton Street, London, W.C.2

Contents

INTRODUCTION   1

THE PEOPLE   5

THE COUNTRY   23

CHURCH AND PALACE, TOWN AND CITY   29

LOVE, COURTSHIP AND MARRIAGE   45

AT WAR   59

RELIGION   81

FEAST DAY AND FIESTA   91

WITH PEN AND BRUSH   105

SONG AND DANCE   125

THE BULLFIGHT   138

CUSTOMS AND IDIOSYNCRASIES   151

FOOD AND DRINK .   161

TRAVELLERS IN SPAIN   170

ACKNOWLEDGEMENTS   182

FOR SUE

Not all the blood at Talavera shed,
Not all the marvels of Barossa's fight,
Not Albuera lavish of the dead,
Have won for Spain her well asserted right.
When shall her Olive-Branch be free from blight?
When shall she breathe her from the blushing toil?
How many a doleful day shall sink in night,
Ere the Frank robber turn him from his spoil,
And Freedome's stranger-tree grow native of the soil.

LORD BYRON

This, the most romantic, racy, and peculiar country of Europe, may in reality be visited by sea and land, and throughout its length and breadth, with ease and safety, as all who have ever been there well know, the nonsense with which Cockney critics who never have been there scare delicate writers in albums and lady-bird tourists, to the contrary notwithstanding: the steamers are regular, the mails and diligences excellent, the roads decent, and the mules surefooted; nay, latterly, the *posadas*, or inns, have been so increased, and the robbers so decreased, that some ingenuity must be evinced in getting either starved or robbed.

RICHARD FORD

Introduction

The English have always been disturbed by Spain and the Spanish. Perhaps they have found it an affront that a country and people so different from themselves should exist, and exist quite satisfactorily, only a few hundred miles away. Whatever the explanation, they have in turn been astonished, frightened, made angry, or become wildly and uncritically enthusiastic about Spanish things. I cannot pretend to be an exception.

My earliest contacts with Spain were a toy bull-fighting set, brought for me from Barcelona, and a child's edition of *Don Quixote*. Neither of these was what it should be. The bullfighters, with their absurd cloaks, could not possibly be put beside the 11th Hussars, my favourite regiment at the time, and weren't even a worthwhile enemy. As for the ridiculous Don Quixote, charging windmills, how could one hope that he would win on the last page? Both filled me with the anger and guilt of unappreciated presents.

The first time I went to Spain was in 1946, when the war was hardly over. And the part I saw was around Gibraltar, the arse end of Europe, as the ship's padre described it to me. It certainly wasn't typical of Spain, or even of Andalusia; and the Spanish were then poorer, and the regime more obviously dictatorial than they seem now. Even so it was a place in a different category from the others one visited in wartime. It is difficult to remember exactly what it was that cast this romantic spell, the café life, the music, the limitless cheap sherry, the frogs and crickets in the warm spring nights. It is a spell from which I have never completely escaped.

Ultimately, of course, it is not the obviously attractive things one finds in Spain, but the Spanish themselves whom one—likes, admires, neither of these is quite the right word, because in English there is no translation for *simpático* that does not give the wrong flavour.

They are at once so childish and so adult, and so totally unashamed of being either. They are the antithesis of the English and though it is an easy and obvious thing to be pleased by what is different and unfamiliar, I think it is not something to hide. By their side the English seem pale, half alive people, persistent, tolerant, industrious—virtues which one finds it easier to admire than like. The influence of the puritan is everywhere and it is natural that, as soon as we go to Spain, we should feel not just relief to escape from this, and delight in superficial Spanish gaiety, but the excitement of a revelation that life can be measured by different standards.

It is how the Spanish live that I have tried to give some picture of in this collection. Visitors, and the Spanish themselves, have seen this in many different ways. They have admired, laughed and been made angry; but they have never been disinterested.

Every visitor to Spain is tempted to write about it— I have an unpublished novel set there—and it is mainly out of the writings of visitors to Spain that I have made my choice. From Dr Andrew Boorde, a fifteenth-century pilgrim, to George Orwell, a twentieth-century crusader, from Nelson, Disraeli and the Duke of Wellington to Hemingway, Rose Macaulay and Sacheverell Sitwell they have left their delighted, shocked, critical or enthusiastic impressions. For a number it has been a transforming experience in their lives. To me they give a better idea of Spain than the writings of the Spanish themselves, not only because they share my own outside point of view, but because they all convey their feelings of discovery and wonder.

They have written about its customs, which always seem a hundred years out of date, and about its countryside, more African than European. They have admired its great buildings and patronized its art, fought for and against its soldiers, had their stomachs excited or upset by its garlicky food and strong wine and their bones rattled together by its roads. They have been astonished by its love and courtship customs and by the whole semi-oriental relationship between men and women. They have taken violent sides about its religion, its politics—and, of course, its bullfights.

2

Roughly, very roughly, I have put my pieces under these headings. But in Spain the Church has made the fiesta, built many of the buildings and as often as not sponsored—or supressed—the art. And it is at the fiesta that you hear the music and frequently see the bullfight. Religion is as hopelessly intertwined with war as it is with marriage. And these, with the national food and drink and many other customs and idiosyncrasies, are only a reflection of the Spanish countryside and of the Spanish themselves. So if my sections overlap it is partly because the task of separating them would be impossible and partly because I would not like them to seem too separate.

From all that has been written it has been hard to select, and I have followed what must be the anthologist's only guide, his own taste. I can only hope that what has excited, amused or moved me, or given me a better understanding of Spain and the Spanish may do the same for others.

Among very many friends who have given me help and advice and lent me books, I should like to thank Isabel Quigly, Martin Seymour-Smith, Charles Hodgson, J. M. Cohen, Christian Ramsay Fairfax, Jaspar Ridley, David Unwin and Peter Grant. In particular I must thank John Haycraft for his many suggestions and comments, for reading the manuscript and for his enthusiasm and encouragement throughout.

T. H.

The People

It is absurd, of course, to generalize about a nation from the sight of two people on a railway platform; but we are travellers —let us correct one generalization by adding a great many more.

V. S. PRITCHETT

It is a temptation we all happily give way to. The less we see, the more whistle-stop our tour, the more ready we are to sum up and hold forth. And a good thing too, because a long study of such a complex and self-contradictory subject as the Spanish character would, or at least should, reduce us to a wise silence.

Absurd as it may be, few have done it so successfully as V. S. Pritchett himself. In 1951 and 1952 he revisited Spain after sixteen years—and a civil war. Here he is at the frontier.

A SIMPLE MATTER

Hendaye: the train dies in the customs. One gets a whiff of Spanish impossibility here. A young Spaniard is at the carriage window talking to a friend who is on the platform; what mightn't he be smuggling. The gendarme tells him to go. The Spaniard notes this and says what he has to say to his friend. It is a simple matter.

"If you go over to see them on Wednesday tell them I have arrived and will come at the end of the week." But if a bossy French gendarme thinks that is how a Spaniard proceeds, he is wrong. The simple idea comes out in this fashion:

"Suppose you see them, tell them I am here, but if not, not; you may not actually see them, but talk to them, on the telephone perhaps, or send a message by someone else and if not on Wednesday, well then Tuesday or Monday, if you have the car you could run over and choose your day and say you saw me, you met me on the station, and I said, if you had some means of sending them a message or you saw them, that I might come over, on Friday, say, or Saturday at the end of the week, say

5

Sunday. Or not. If I come there I come, but if not, we shall see, so that supposing you see them . . ." Two Spaniards can keep up this kind of thing for an hour; one has only to read their newspapers to see they are wrapped in a cocoon of prolixity. The French gendarme repeats that the Spaniard must leave. The Spaniard on the platform turns his whole body, not merely his head, and looks without rancour at the gendarme. The Spaniard is considering a most difficult notion—the existence of a personality other than his own. He turns back, for he has failed to be aware of anything more than a blur of opposition. It is not resented. Simply, he is incapable of doing more than one thing at a time. Turning to the speaker in the train, he goes over the same idea from his point of view, in the same detail, adding personal provisos and subclauses, until a kind of impenetrable web has been woven round both parties. They are aware of nothing but their individual selves, and the very detail of their talk is a method of defeating any awareness of each other. They are lost in the sound of their own humming, monotonous egos and only a bullet could wake them out of it.

These are the people of Madrid as he remembers them in the 'thirties.

SINGLE-PURPOSE MEN

In this period Madrid produced—and it still produces—a large number of what can only be called single-purpose men or Oblomovs. A number of these might have the occupation of remaining in bed all day and would rise at six merely to fulfil the function of walking; others were devoted chiefly to sleep— I remember a pleasant Marquis, a very intelligent man, who must have been the aesthete of sleep, the Walter Pater of the long torpid moment. Another I remember was a gambler, another a pursuer of women; many were full-time talkers. Some sat alone. These were their occupations, their entire life. In one Andalusian town there was a man called "the night-husband", an unhappy man who had two illegitimate families besides his own—an Andalusian habit that is a throwback to the harem system copied from the Moors—and who was therefore known "to be unable to be about in the daytime". Others were journalists who went to an office to talk, but who never wrote; many were contact men, who walked the streets in order to scrape acquaintance and hope for a commission to turn up. A large number of civil servants notoriously appeared at their offices only on pay day. These single-purpose men were not necessarily rich. They had some small rent, perhaps, and, having the Spanish instinct for frugal living and for finding the basic

6

minimum of human need and effort, could live on that or
perhaps on the subvention of an unprotesting relative. In every
family there seemed to be one phenomenal man whose single
function it unluckily was to work day and night, often at two
or three different professions, so that he might be a solicitor for
one part of the day, a civil servant at some other or an agent for
a company, and in the evenings a journalist and a teacher. It
was he who supported, without complaint, a large family of his
own and a number of relations whose special gift happened to
be the one of doing without regular employment. And even
these workers had found a minimum; they had discovered
quite naturally how to live on a minimum of pleasure.

Franco's victory has given a longer lease to the single-purpose
man. . . .

The Spanish Temper, 1954

If the Spanish character is elusive, one good reason is
that Spain, more than any other country of Western
Europe, is still an arbitrary collection of separate
provinces, each with its separate people. In the early
'twenties Arturo Barea was an engineering sergeant
with the Spanish Army in Morocco during its dis-
illusioning war against Abd-el-Krim.

A BARE HUNDRED MILES

I learned about the races of Spain by dealing with the ship-
ments of recruits. . . .

The ship moored, the gangplank was fixed, and they began to
stream out of the boat, mostly land-workers and labourers from
all parts of Spain. There were the Andalusians in their short,
light jackets, white or khaki, often in shirt-sleeves, their
trousers held in place by string or a sash. Most of them were
slim and straight, dark, sallow, gipsy-like, with black eyes
opening in mingled apprehension and curiosity, talking quickly
in a torrent of obscene swear-words.

There were the men from the Castilian plains and sierras,
taciturn, small, bony, tanned by sun, wind, frost and snow, the
legs of their corduroy trousers fastened with twine over their
bulging pants which in their turn were tied with tape over thick,
blue or red, home-knitted socks. Every now and again the whole
formation would be upset because a man's tape-ends had come
untied.

Basques, Gallegos and Asturians usually came in a mixed lot
on the same ship, and their discrepancies were astounding. The
huge Basques, in blue blouses, with the inevitable beret on the

crown of their small heads, were serious and silent, and if they spoke in that incomprehensible language of theirs, they measured their words. You felt the strength of their individual being and of their self-contained culture. The Gallegos came mostly from poor, forlorn villages; they used to be incredibly dirty, often barefoot, and they faced this new affliction, worse than the familiar penury at home, with a bovine resignation. The Asturians from the mountains were strong and agile, great gluttons and bawdy merry-makers, and they mocked at the wretchedness of the people from Galicia, as well as at the gravity of the Basques.

Then there arrived pot-bellied, black, old transatlantic steamers with a load of recruits from the Mediterranean provinces, from Catalonia, parts of Aragon, Valencia and Alicante. The mountain people from Aragon and northern Catalonia differed in language, but they were much alike, primitive, harsh, and almost savage. The Catalans from the ports, in contact with all the Mediterranean civilization, were a world apart from their countrymen of the mountains. The people of the Levante, in black blouses and laced *alpargatas*, rather handsome, but lymphatic and flabby with the promise of an early paunch, were a group by themselves.

And it seemed to me that a Madrileño is less of a stranger to a New Yorker than a Basque is to a Gallego, with their villages a bare hundred miles apart.

The Track, 1943

The proud Spaniard is proverbial. Because this pride does not depend on status or prosperity but on being a Spaniard, there is a natural democracy about Spanish society which it is easier for Americans than the class-conscious English to understand. In Restoration times Lady Anne Fanshawe went with her husband, Sir Richard, to Madrid where he was Ambassador.

THE QUALITY

They are civil to all as their qualities require, with the highest respect, so that I have seen a grandee and a duke . . . put off his hat to the meanest woman that makes a reverence, though it be their footman's wife. They meddle with no neighbour's fortune or person, but their own families; and they are punctual in visits, men to men, and women to women.

LADY ANNE FANSHAWE *Memoirs*

I try never to travel without a Baedeker, preferably an

ON THE COSTA BLANCA

*His fishing days are past, but he still
takes an academic interest in the catch*

BAR SUPPORTER

*Where shall I be this time the year after next? A bar's
a bar even if it is neon-lit, chromium-plated, half-devoted
to sticky biscuits and set in a suburb like a bomb site*

edition of the eighteen nineties or early nineteen hundreds, with its charming lapses from the works of the masters to the practical: "Ladies mind the step." More than fifty years old though they may be, it is surprising how much relevant advice they give.

INTERCOURSE WITH THE PEOPLE

In educated circles the stranger is at first apt to be carried away by the lively, cheerful, and obliging tone of society, by the charming spontaneity of manner, and by the somewhat exaggerated politeness of the people he meets. He should, however, avoid turning the conversation on serious matters, and should above all refrain from expressing an opinion on religious or political questions. The national pride of the Spaniard and his ignorance of foreign conditions renders a collision in such cases almost inevitable. . . .

The Spaniard of the lower classes is not devoid of national pride, but he possesses much more common sense and a much healthier dislike of humbug than his so-called superiors. The tactful stranger will not find it difficult to get in touch with him. Two points, however, must be carefully remembered. In the first place it is necessary to maintain a certain courtesy of manner towards even the humblest individual, who always expects to be treated as a "caballero". In the second place the traveller, while maintaining his rights with quiet decision, should avoid all rudeness or roughness, which simply serves to excite the inflammable passions of the uneducated Spaniard.

BAEDEKER'S *Spain and Portugal*, 1908

Of all writers on Spain, I find Richard Ford the most continuously entertaining and vivacious. In fact his *Handbook for Spain* was so entertaining that his friend Addington, British Minister at Madrid, persuaded him to withdraw the first edition and issue an expurgated one, which he did in 1855. Fortunately most of the supressed matter reappeared soon afterwards in his *Gatherings from Spain*.

YOUR SPANISH SERVANT

In general, a firm, quiet, courteous, and somewhat reserved manner is most effective. Whenever duties are to be performed, let them see that you are not to be trifled with. The coolness of a determined Englishman's manner, when in earnest, is what few foreigners can withstand. . . . An Englishman, without being over-familiar, may venture on a far greater degree of unbending in his intercourse with his Spanish dependents than he can dare to do with those he has in England. It is the custom of the country; they are used to it, and their heads are not turned by it, nor do they ever forget their relative positions. The Spaniards treat their servants very much like the ancient Romans or the modern Moors; they are more their *vernae*, their domestic slaves. It is the absolute authority of the father combined with kindness.

Colonel T. P. Melvill knew the Spanish aristocracy between the World Wars, at a time when Alfonso XIII was still a ruling king.

THE OLD ARISTOCRACY

As a polo player and a member of the British Embassy—I purposely put them in that order—I was admitted and welcomed into the tiny and exclusive circle of the Spanish Aristocracy, where the old-world traditions still survived, with a distinct flavour of the eighteenth century. They were the only people I have come across, who, if I slapped them on the back and said "Do you know I thought you were an Englishman?" were *not* pleased.

Ponies and Women, 1932

From personal pride follows Spanish local pride. The Spaniard is proud, not just of his province but of his own small town (*pueblo*). It is better than all others.

THE PUEBLO

Each pueblo possesses a collection of ballads recording local history, and of sayings and rhymes in which the praises of the pueblo are sung and derogatory observations are made of its neighbours. . . . A rhyme inspired by the same spirit can usually be found for any pueblo, and I give one which is known in Alcalá:

En el pueblo de Zahara	"In the pueblo of Zahara
Hay dos cosas regulares	There are two things which aren't up to much
Una p'arriba y una p'abajo	One in the upper town and one in the lower
Y en medio los mula'res.	And in between are the dung-heaps."

In the folklore of its neighbours Alcalá is represented in a similar light, but within the pueblo its name is heard only in the most complimentary contexts. A ballad recounts how a visiting official was outwitted and put to shame by the noble people of that place, and a more ancient saying tells that after the Resurrection the Saviour stopped off on his way to Heaven at the *calvario* of Alcalá, a signal honour which has afforded the inhabitants special protection ever since from the damage wrought by thunderstorms. In a rhyme the excellence of Alcalá is contrasted with the wretchedness of its neighbours:

El Jaral corral de cabras	"El Jaral is a pen for she-goats
Guadalmesí de cabritos	Guadalmesí for kids
Benalurín de cabrones	Benalurín for he-goats
Y Alcalá de señoritos.	And Alcalá for gentlemen."

The most proud saying of all comes from the town of Jimena, which challenges the rest of the world in terms of piteous contempt:

Ay! que pena	"What a shame!
No ser de Jimena!	Not to be from Jimena!"

But, typically, the neighbouring pueblos have found a line to add:

Y arrastrarse el culo en la arena.	
"And drag your arse along in the sand."	

For the people of Jimena enjoy a local reputation for being short in the leg.

J. A. PITT-RIVERS *The People of the Sierra*, 1954

From local pride follows national pride.

ADAM'S VISIT

It was but the other day that a foreigner was relating in a *tertulia* or conversazione of Madrid, the well known anecdote of Adam's revisit to earth. The narrator explained how our first father on lighting in Italy was perplexed and taken aback; how, on crossing the Alps into Germany, he found nothing that he could understand—how matters got darker and stranger at Paris, until on his reaching England he was altogether lost, confounded, and abroad, being unable to make out any thing. Spain was his next point, where, to his infinite satisfaction, he

11

found himself quite at home, so little had things changed since his absence, or indeed since the sun at its creation first shone over Toledo. The story concluded, a distinguished Spaniard, who was present, hurt perhaps at the somewhat protestant-dissenting tone of the speaker, gravely remarked, the rest of the party coinciding,—"Sí, Señor, y tenía razón; la España es Paradiso"—"Adam, Sir, was right, for Spain is paradise."

RICHARD FORD *Gatherings from Spain*, 1861

If Spanish pride is proverbial, so is Spanish idealism, with its lost-cause, Quixotic flavour.

OF THE VALOROUS DON QUIXOTE'S SUCCESS IN THE DREADFUL
AND NEVER BEFORE IMAGINED ADVENTURE OF THE WINDMILLS
WITH OTHER EVENTS WORTHY OF HAPPY RECORD

At that moment they caught sight of some thirty or forty windmills, which stand on that plain, and as soon as Don Quixote saw them he said to his squire: "Fortune is guiding our affairs better than we could have wished. Look over there, friend Sancho Panza, where more than thirty monstrous giants appear. I intend to do battle with them and take all their lives. With their spoils we will begin to get rich, for this is a fair war, and it is a great service to God to wipe such a wicked brood from the face of the earth."

"What giants?" asked Sancho Panza.

"Those you see there," replied his master, "with their long arms. Some giants have them about six miles long."

"Take care, your worship," said Sancho; "those things over there are not giants but windmills, and what seem to be their arms are the sails, which are whirled round in the wind and make the millstone turn."

"It is quite clear," replied Don Quixote, "that you are not experienced in this matter of adventures. They are giants, and if you are afraid, go away and say your prayers, whilst I advance and engage them in fierce and unequal battle."

As he spoke, he dug his spurs into his steed Rocinante, paying no attention to his squire's shouted warning that beyond all doubt they were windmills and no giants he was advancing to attack. But he went on, so positive that they were giants that he neither listened to Sancho's cries nor noticed what they were, even when he got near them. Instead he went on shouting in a loud voice: "Do not fly, cowards, vile creatures, for it is one knight alone who assails you."

At that moment a slight wind arose, and the great sails began to move. At the sight of which Don Quixote shouted: "Though you wield more arms than the giant Briareus, you shall pay for it!" Saying this, he commended himself with all his soul to his Lady Dulcinea, beseeching her aid in his great peril. Then, covering himself with his shield and putting his lance in the rest, he urged Rocinante forward at a full gallop and attacked the nearest windmill, thrusting his lance into the sail. But the wind turned it with such violence that it shivered his weapon in pieces, dragging the horse and rider with it, and sent the knight rolling badly injured across the plain. Sancho Panza rushed to his assistance as fast as his ass could trot, but when he came up he found that the knight could not stir. Such a shock had Rocinante given him in their fall.

"Oh my goodness!" cried Sancho. "Didn't I tell your worship to look what you were doing, for they were only windmills? Nobody could mistake them, unless he had windmills on the brain."

"Silence, friend Sancho," replied Don Quixote. "Matters of war are more subject than most to continual chance. What is more, I think—and that is the truth—that the same sage Friston who robbed me of my room and my books has turned those giants into windmills, to cheat me of the glory of conquering them. Such is the enmity he bears me; but in the very end his black arts shall avail him little against the goodness of my sword."

"God send it as He will," replied Sancho Panza, helping the knight to get up and remount Rocinante, whose shoulders were half dislocated.

MIGUEL DE CERVANTES SAAVEDRA *Don Quixote*, 1605.
Trans. J. M. Cohen

But what is there idealistic about that other great and traditional Spanish character, Don Juan? At dawn one morning on our honeymoon, during a small town fiesta, my wife went for a ride into the country on a white donkey with eight young Spaniards, one of them, of course, a bullfighter. They were gay, friendly, until they came to a barn where she had to fight to get out and run all the way home through maize fields. She told me about it when I woke up for breakfast.

John Haycraft ran a language school in Cordoba and this was one of his pupils.

DON JUAN

I remember a bank clerk who prided himself on being a Don Juan. Sometimes he would excuse himself from classes because a woman from Madrid was coming down to visit him. Afterwards, he would indulge in detailed descriptions of the delights which missing an English lesson could afford. Before we had had two classes, he asked me the English equivalents of innumerable Spanish obscenities, and when we met in the street would discharge these with carefree delight, to the wonder of passing tourists, so that I began to feel rather as if I had presented a small child with a loaded six-shooter. However, some months after I first met him, he told me that all his ladies were paid for and that he had to use drugs.

Babel in Spain, 1958

Don Juan has had many interpreters, and though I prefer to take a less analytical view than the following I include it to complete the picture.

ON THE COUCH

In recent years Don Juan has met his worst enemy—the psychologists. They find him to be not the mature and energetic man, but the infantile male, possibly homosexual, possibly almost impotent or with a neurotic fear of incapacity. He is fixed in the undifferentiated sexuality of adolescence. He is a myth created for those thousands of penniless lonely Spanish males who walk up and down the streets all night, who never see a woman outside their own homes, who are dominated by the all-powerful figure of the Spanish mother. Hundreds of these unstrenuous dreamers of love are supposed, in Madrid, to get their mild satisfactions from being crushed against the girls in the trams at the rush hour. The tramway lovers they are called.

v. s. PRITCHETT *The Spanish Temper*

What about Spanish cruelty? Or Spanish courtesy? In the end it seems not merely that most possible qualities have been attributed to the Spanish, but that they have become renowned for each. Even cunning—though Franco, of course, is a Gallego.

HITLER AND FRANCO

Franco's meeting with Hitler at Hendaye in October 1940 was one of the comical incidents of the war. It was a meeting between northern romance, gesture, and vagueness with Spanish evasiveness and precision. After it Hitler said that rather than go through another interview with Franco he would sooner have three or four teeth out. Hitler came for his reward for having supported General Franco in the Civil War; the General asked for large pieces of French Africa, Gibraltar, and also for food and oil. The last was the vital thing for a Spain that was broken and starving; Hitler could not supply them and not even the bait of capturing Gibraltar would tempt the General. When it comes down to a question of necessity, the Spaniards do not really want Gibraltar; they wants its nuisance value.

V. S. PRITCHETT The Spanish Temper

If Spanish men are a self-contradictory mixture, the women seem more consistent. The beautiful but protected girl, whose life is devoted to catching a husband, becomes the matriarch, controlling husband and family. As Pritchett says, "there is marriage and eight children in their eyes". To Havelock Ellis they seemed so dominating that he suggested that Spain's great wars of conquest had killed off so many of her best men that the race now automatically bred superior women.

But if the beautiful Spanish girl is the potential matriarch, this has made her no less diverting to visitors. I well remember, one evening in La Linea, pulling a hesitating friend back into the street while a gold-toothed, dark-haired girl wriggled and pulled him towards an inner room. What surprised me more than the girl or the bed beyond the doorway was the old mother who sat in the front room, watching everything but never saying a word.

In the early nineteenth century two young Englishmen, to become much better known, visited southern Spain, each on his way to the Orient. Each wrote home.

THESE ESPAGNOLAS

You know that I am rather an admirer of the blonde; and, to be perfectly candid, I will confess to you that the only times which I have been so unfortunate as to be captivated, or captured, in this country were both by Englishwomen. But these Espagnolas are nevertheless very interesting personages. . . . The general female dress in this country is a black silk, called a <i>basquiña</i>, and a black silk shawl, with which they usually envelop their head, called a <i>mantilla</i>. As they walk along in this costume in an evening, with their soft dark

15

eyes dangerously conspicuous, you willingly believe in their universal beauty. They are remarkable for the beauty of their hair; of this they are very proud, and indeed its luxuriance is only equalled by the attention which they lavish on its culture. I have seen a young girl of fourteen whose hair reached her feet. . . . All day long, even the lowest order are brushing, curling, and arranging it. A fruit-woman has her hair dressed with as much care as the Duchess of Ossuna. At this time of the year they do not wear the mantilla generally over the head, but show their combs, which are of immense size. The fashion of their combs varies constantly, every two or three months, though the part of the costume of which the Spanish female is most proud. The moment that a new comb appears, even the servant wench will have her old one melted down, and thus, with the cost of a dollar or two, appear the next holiday in the newest style. These combs are worn at the back of the head. They are of tortoiseshell, the very fashionable wear them of white. I sat next to a lady of high distinction at a bull-fight at Seville. She was the daughter-in-law of the Captain-General, and the most beautiful Spaniard I have yet met. Her comb was white, and she wore a mantilla of blonde, I have no doubt extremely valuable, for it was very dirty. The effect, however, was charming. Her hair was glossy black, and her eye like an antelope's, but all her other features deliciously soft; and she was further adorned, which is rare in Spain, with a rosy cheek, for here our heroines are rather sallow. But they counteract this defect by never appearing until twilight, which calls them from their bowers, fresh, though languid, from the late siesta. . . .

I generally sleep for two hours. I think this practice conducive to health. Old people, however, are apt to carry it to excess. By the time I have risen and arranged my toilette it is time to steal out, and call upon any agreeable family whose Tertullia you may choose to honour, which you do, after the first time, uninvited, and with them you take your tea or chocolate. This is often *al fresco*, under the piazza or colonnade of the *patio*. Here you while away the time until it is cool enough for the *alameda* or public walk. At Cadiz, and even at Seville . . . you are sure of a delightful breeze from the water. The sea breeze comes like a spirit. The effect is quite magical. As you are lolling in listless languor in the hot and perfumed air, an invisible guest comes dancing into the party and touches them all with an enchanted wand. All start, all smile. It has come; it is the sea breeze. There is much discussion whether it is as strong, or whether weaker, than the night before. The ladies furl their fans and seize their mantillas, the cavaliers stretch their legs and give signs of life. All rise. I offer my arm to Dolores or Florentina (is not this familiarity strange?), and in ten minutes you are in the *alameda*. What a change! All is now life and liveliness. Such bowing, such kissing, such fluttering of fans, such gentle criticism of gentle friends! But the fan is the most wonderful part of the whole scene. A Spanish lady with her fan might shame the tactics of a troop of horse. Now she unfurls it with the slow pomp and conscious elegance of a peacock. Now she flutters it with all the languor of a listless beauty, now with all the liveliness of a vivacious one. Now, in the midst of a very tornado, she closes it with a whir which makes you start, pop! In the midst of your confusion Dolores taps you on the elbow; you turn round to listen, and Florentina pokes you in your side. Magical instrument. You know that it speaks a particular language, and gallantry requires no other mode to express its most subtle conceits or its most unreasonable demands than this slight, delicate organ. But remember, while you read, that here, as in England, it is not confined alone to your delightful sex. I also have my fan, which makes my cane extremely jealous. If you think I have grown extraordinarily effeminate, learn that in this scorching climate the soldier will not mount guard without one. Night wears on, we sit, we take a *panal*, which is as quick work as snapdragon, and far more elegant; again we stroll. Midnight clears the public walks, but few Spanish families retire till two. A solitary bachelor like myself still wanders, or still lounges on a bench in the warm moonlight. The last guitar dies away, the cathedral clock wakes up your reverie, you too seek your couch, and amid a gentle, sweet flow of loveliness, and light, and music, and fresh air, thus dies a day in Spain.

BENJAMIN DISRAELI Letter to his mother, Granada, 1830

AN EXCHANGE OF LOCKS

We lodged in the house of two Spanish unmarried ladies, who possess *six* houses in Seville, and gave me a curious specimen of Spanish manners. They are women of character, and the eldest a fine woman, the youngest pretty, but not so good a figure as Donna Josepha. The freedom of manner, which is general here, astonished me not a little; and in the course of further observation, I find that reserve is not the characteristic of Spanish belles, who are, in general, very handsome, with large black eyes, and very fine forms. The eldest honoured your *unworthy* son with very particular attention, embracing him with great tenderness at parting (I was there but three days), after cutting off a lock of his hair, and presenting him with one of her own, about three feet in length, which I send, and beg you will retain till my return. Her last words were, *Adios, tu hermoso! me gusto mucho*—"Adieu, you pretty fellow! you please me much." She offered me a share of her apartment, which my *virtue* induced me to decline; she laughed, and said I had some English *amante* (lover), and added that she was going to be married to an officer in the Spanish army. . . .

I beg leave to observe that intrigue here is the business of life; when a woman marries she throws off all restraint, but I believe their conduct is chaste enough before. If you make a proposal, which in England will bring a box on the ear from the meekest of virgins, to a Spanish girl, she thanks you for the honour you intend her, and replies, "Wait till I am married, and I shall be too happy." This is literally and strictly true.

LORD BYRON Letter to his mother, Gibraltar, 1809

Other visitors have been less tolerant.

WOMEN OF CÁDIZ

Presuming upon their charms, the ladies of this city indulge in some curious whims. Every family of any consequence has a state-bed, highly ornamented, and placed in an elegantly fitted-up apartment and the use made of it is this: at a particular time of the year, generally after Lent, the *señora* of the house, or her daughter, if she has reached and her mother has passed a certain age, feigns sickness. Having previously made all the necessary arrangements, she takes to her bed; there she lies in an elegant nightdress, under embroidered sheets, her head resting upon a rose-coloured silk pillow, and a tablestand near her with silver candlesticks and wax lights, a little silver bell, and several vases containing choice perfumes. There she receives company; there all her male and female acquaintances resort, and there, attired to be seen and bent upon admiration, she listens to the language of mock condolence, pleasing flattery and undisguised gallantry!

I was informed that the ladies of Cádiz are adepts in the manufacture of the female person; that in looking at them, we may frequently apply with truth the well-known proverb "all is not gold that glitters", and that the most experienced dressmaker of the British metropolis would be "all in amaze" at the various and subtle uses to which the cork tree is put in the City of Cádiz.

HENRY D. INGLIS *Spain in 1830*

It is, of course, at Seville that the legendary black-haired, dark-eyed, carnation-wearing Spanish girl can still be seen.

AT THE FERIA

Taking the young women first, there are the two sorts, those who go pillion and those who ride alone. The pillion riders, perched precariously with an arm round their partner's waist or holding to the horse's tail, wear the flounced skirts of the pedestrians. Their brothers, or lovers, ride generally one arm akimbo, which accentuates their thin waists. Many are wearing elaborate and fanciful leather trousers, in which we can see the origin of the cowboys' leggings and of the Mexican *charro* costume. The young women ride pillion with an amazing grace, the beauty of their bare heads and arms in that violet sunlight being as animal as the steeds they share. Every young woman is beautiful to look at, some of the girls being real visions of Spanish beauty with their camellia skins and black hair and eyes. But not all are dark, and there are young girls riding pillion, in green or white crinolines, with fair hair, bareheaded like the rest, and glowing in the midday sun.

It is wonderful to watch a cavalier, arm akimbo, riding towards us, Spanish-fashion, and then to wait and admire the young woman upon the crupper holding lightly to his waist. But the other sort of riders, the true Amazons, are yet more enthralling, those who ride by themselves, astride, not hatless, and wearing more than one type of costume; in fact, one form of dress is worn the first day of the Feria, and . . . tomorrow they will be wearing another costume and a different form of headdress. The first . . . consists of a leather apron and divided skirt, a white shirt like a man's, a short jacket, and one of the hard-brimmed Córdoban hats. It is a feminine version of what the men are wearing, with the addition perhaps of a rose behind the ear. The thin waist, the level shoulders and hard outline of the hat, worn at a charming angle above a rounded face, such are the attractions of this riding dress, which is infinitely varied in detail and which suits the Spanish type of good looks to perfection.

The other form of costume belongs, as it were, to another tradition; the shirt or trousers, it matters not which, are not so aggressively in imitation of the masculine; the jacket is short, and without the leather apron or leggings is more revealing of the figure; the hair is worn at the back in a snood or chignon, while the hat is a round black one, resembling the crown, without the wings, of the matador's three-cornered cap or tricorne. This must, undoubtedly, be its inspiration, and nothing more in the popular tradition of Spain could be imagined than a young woman on horseback in one of these round black hats, particularly if she be wearing, instead of a snood, a *mantilla de madronos*, which is a scarlet or magenta net with wide meshes worked with bobbles. The soft complexions of the young girls are ravishing to behold, and to compare with the carnation or camellia behind the ear, to which we must add the peculiar beauties of the Spanish horsemanship that allow of so graceful a seat and, where the woman riders are concerned, could have been conceived especially in order to be admired.

SACHEVERELL SITWELL *Spain*, 1950

It is nearly 500 years since the fall of Granada to Ferdinand and Isabel, and the final defeat of the Moors. How much Moorish blood remains?

AXA, FÁTIMA, AND MARIÉN

Three Moorish girls I loved
In Jaén,
Axa and Fátima and Marién.

Three Moorish girls so gay
Went olive-plucking there,
And found them plucked away
In Jaén,
Axa and Fátima and Marién.

And found them plucked away
And turned back in dismay,
And pale and sad were they
In Jaén,
Axa and Fátima and Marién.

Three Moorish girls so fair,
Three Moorish girls so fair
Went apple-plucking there
In Jaén,
Axa and Fátima and Marién.

ANON., fifteenth century
Trans. JEAN ROGERS LONGLAND

How much of the tradition comes from another exotic source?

GYPSY WOMEN

There is a word in the Gypsy language to which those who
speak it attach ideas of peculiar reverence, far superior to that
connected with the name of the Supreme Being, the creator of
themselves and the universe. This word is *Lácha*, which with
them is the corporeal chastity of the females; we say corporeal
chastity, for no other do they hold in the slightest esteem; it is
lawful amongst them, nay praiseworthy, to be obscene in look,
gesture, and discourse, to be accessories to vice, and to stand
by and laugh at the worst abominations of the Busné, provided
their *Lácha ye trupos*, or corporeal chastity, remains unblem-
ished. The Gypsy child, from her earliest years is told by her
strange mother, that a good Calli need only dread one thing
in this world, and that is the loss of Lácha, in comparison with
which that of life is of little consequence, as in such an event
she will be provided for, but what provision is there for a
Gypsy who has lost her Lácha? "Bear this in mind, my child,"
she will say, "and now eat this bread, and go forth and see
what you can steal."

GEORGE BORROW *The Zincali*, 1841

In Charles II's reign Pepys was sent to supervise the
destruction and evacuation of Tangier—I can always
spend an inconclusive five minutes speculating about
what would have happened if England had kept a
second Gibraltar in Africa. On his way home, busy as
usual, he called on Spain and had time to make a few
pungent notes on Spanish life—and Spanish women.

NOTES ON SPAIN

No chamber-pots in all the country, the weather being warm
and drinking too little to need a pot in the night. . . .

No man will praise a woman, or woman a man, or anything
else without a blowing at the end of it, for fear of hurting it
(unknown to themselves) with the mal de ojo, by their over
affection to it. . . .

Won't piss in the streets, but doors.

Mothers will help their sons and daughters in evil, and
neither father nor mother think it ill to hear of their son's
going a-whoring.

The severest women all the year will hear and talk and almost
do anything for three days before Lent, and their husbands
bear it.

The Tangier Papers of Samuel Pepys

21

It is as organizers of the lives of their husbands and families that Spanish women are at their most typical, and formidable. Here is a nineteenth-century English diplomat's analysis of how the country was really governed.

PETTICOAT INFLUENCE

This is the general system in Spain, and petticoat influence has in consequence by far the most preponderating weight in affairs. Does a person wish to obtain any situation, post, or office, to be appointed to a certain command, or to effect, in short, any object essential to his interest and of which the government has the disposal, his rib, as a far abler negotiator than himself, is despatched to Madrid and, repairing every day to the minister's levées, brings into play her different points of character and the numberless little tricks which her sex in general, and the Spanish ladies in particular, know so well how to exhibit to the best advantage. A Spanish minister's levée is thus crowded with fair applicants, who bring into play the whole of the artillery with which nature may have supplied them against the crafty courtier. . . . Those who happen to be blessed with any superior share of personal charms and attractions, accompanied with proportionate address, are first attended to and seldom have to wait long, or fail in the object of their mission; the others make up with hard dollars. In the end, they are all sent trotting back to their spouses in the country, tolerably content and not dissatisfied, at least, with the gaieties of the capital which their little trip has thus enabled them to indulge in.

SIR ARTHUR DE CAPELL *The Attaché in Madrid*

PROVERBS

Guárdate de la mala mujer y de la buena no fíes nada.
"Protect yourself from a bad woman and put no trust in a good one."

El consejo de la mujer es poco y el que no lo toma es loco.
"A woman's advice is worth little but he who doesn't take it is mad."

The Country

Ancha es Castilla.
"Castile is broad."

Nueve meses de invierno y tres de infierno.
"Nine months of winter and three of hell."

Tierra de santos y de cantos.
"Land of saints and boulders."
                                        Castilian sayings

Spain is not Castile and when you go there you are more
likely to expect the soft luxuriance of Andalusia, so
powerfully has this image been spread by generations
of romantic writers. Because I first saw Spain from the
south it was some time and several visits before I
realized how dry, unwelcoming and unromantic most
of it is. The more civilized our lives the more we are
drawn to the scenically bleak and of Spain's varied
regions and scenery it is the uplands of Castile I now
find most exciting.

WAY IN—AND WAY OUT

To know what we are up against we ought to go to Spain by
aeroplane and fly to the centre of it. Beneath us England
is packed with little houses, if the earth is visible at all through
the haze; France lies clearly like green linoleum broken into a
small busy pattern, a place of thriving little fields; but, cross the
dark blot of the Pyrenees, and Spain is reddish brown, yellow,
and black, like some dusty bull restive in the rock and the sand
and (we would guess) uninhabited. The river-beds are wide
and bleached dry. After Switzerland this is the highest country
in Europe. The centre is a tableland torn open by gorges, and
on the table the mountain ranges are spaciously disposed.
There is little green, except on the seaboard; or rather the
green is the dark gloss of ilex, olive, and pine, which from the
height at which we are flying appear in lake-like and purple

blobs. For the most part we are looking down at steppe which is iced in the long winter and cindery like a furnace floor in the short summer. Fortified desert—and yet the animal image returns again and again in this metalled and rocky scene, for occasionally some peak will give a sudden upward thrust, like the twist of a bull's horns, at the wings of the plane. Flying over Spain, we wonder at the torture that time had put upon the earth's crust and how human beings can live there. In Soria, the terrible province, below the wicked mountains of Aragón, I remember picking up an old woman who had fallen off her donkey and carrying her to the side of the road and wiping the blood off her nose. She was a figure carved in wood, as light as a husk. It was like having starvation in one's hands.

But it is better, I think, to go the slow way to Spain and to feel the break with Europe at the land frontiers. It is true that at Irún one is not in Spain but in the Basque provinces, among people of mysterious race and language who are an anomaly in Europe; and that, at the other end of the Pyrenees, one is in Catalonia, where the people are really Provençal, speak their own tongue, and scornfully alter the Spanish proverb, "Africa begins at the Pyrenees," into "Africa begins at the Ebro." But the stamp of Spain is on these provinces and the Spanish strain runs over the frontiers. One finds it in Montpellier; on the Atlantic side it reaches into Biarritz, Saint Jean-de-Luz, and Bayonne. And in these towns one meets something profoundly and disturbingly Spanish which goes down to the roots of the Spanish nature: one meets the exiles. For long before the Europe of the 1930s or the Russia of the early nineteenth century, Spain is the great producer of exiles, a country unable to tolerate its own people. The Moors, the Jews, the Protestants, the reformers—out with them; and out, at different periods, with the liberals, the atheists, the priests, the Kings, the presidents, the generals, the socialists, the anarchists, fascists, and communists; out with the Right, out with the Left, out with every government. The fact recalls that cruel roar of abuse that goes up in the ring when the bullfighter misses a trick; out with him. Hendaye and Bayonne are there to remind us that before the dictatorships and police states and witch-hunters of contemporary history, Spain has been imperial in the trade of producing exiles. And the exiles go out over the bridge at Hendaye into France, the country that has tolerated all, and at the windows of the French hotel the new exile stands, looking across the bight of sea at the gloomy belfries of his native country, hears their harsh bells across the water, and hates the France which has given him sanctuary. He is proud of his hatred, sinks into fatalism, apathy, intrigue, quarrels

LOOK WHAT I CAUGHT

*Only he didn't—merely scrounged them on the beach
where the fishermen of Castel de Ferro tip their catches
in the early morning and sell them by auction*

PEASANT WITH MATTOCK

It's still a land of donkey cart and ox plough, of small holdings and hand labour. He won't be allowed to do it this way much longer—and a good thing, no doubt

with all the other exiles, and says with pride: "We are the impossible people."

V. S. PRITCHETT The Spanish Temper

Elizabeth Hamilton describes the landscape of Castile, little changed today from what it was when St Teresa of Avila crossed it with her cavalcade of mules and donkeys.

THE PLAIN OF CASTILE

The plain of Castile reaches on and on, hour after hour. From time to time its monotony is broken by a plantation of evergreen oaks with black, writhing branches. A village is rare as an oasis in a desert and, when it comes, is hardly more than a handful of mud-coloured hovels, clustering as if for protection round a church that looks absurdly large.

There is little sign of life. An eagle hovers, tawny winged, lost in the sky's immensity. A crow with plumage that glints a vivid, metallic blue, rises; then drops again. A shepherd watches over sheep the colour of stones. A rider wearing a wide-brimmed hat reins-in his horse, then shades his eyes to watch the train.

The Great Teresa, 1960

Washington Irving, the great American enthusiast for Spain, gives romantics a warning. His literary reputation has declined since the days when Dickens' pockets were "filled with Irving's books worn to tatters", and Thackeray compared him to Goldsmith, but his understanding of Spain still makes him well worth reading.

A STERN, MELANCHOLY COUNTRY

Many are apt to picture Spain to their imaginations as a soft southern region, decked out with the luxuriant charms of voluptuous Italy. On the contrary, though there are exceptions in some of the maritime provinces, yet, for the greater part, it is a stern, melancholy country, with rugged mountains, and long sweeping plains, destitute of trees, and indescribably silent and lonesome, partaking of the savage and solitary character of Africa. What adds to this silence and loneliness, is the absence of singing-birds, a natural consequence of the want of groves and hedges. The vulture and the eagle are seen wheeling about the mountain-cliffs, and soaring over the plains, and groups of shy bustards stalk about the heaths; but the

25

myriads of smaller birds, which animate the whole face of other countries, are met with in but few provinces in Spain, and in those chiefly among the orchards and gardens which surround the habitations of man.

In the interior provinces the traveller occasionally traverses great tracts cultivated with grain as far as the eye can reach, waving at times with verdure, at other times naked and sunburnt, but he looks round in vain for the hand that has tilled the soil. At length he perceives some village on a steep hill, or rugged crag, with mouldering battlements and ruined watchtower: a stronghold, in old times, against civil war, or Moorish inroad: for the custom among the peasantry of congregating together for mutual protection is still kept up in most parts of Spain, in consequence of the maraudings of roving freebooters.

But though a great part of Spain is deficient in the garniture of groves and forests, and the softer charms of ornamental cultivation, yet its scenery is noble in its severity and in unison with the attributes of its people; and I think that I better understand the proud, hardy, frugal, and abstemious Spaniard, his manly defiance of hardships, and contempt of effeminate indulgences, since I have seen the country he inhabits.

The Alhambra, 1832

But south we must go with the northerner's longing for sun and yet more sun. So thoroughly am I conditioned by the popular image that when I have visited Spain but not reached Andalusia I have had the feeling that I have not really been there.

ANDALUSIA

Andalusia is a country of roses and giant violets, jasmine and orange blossom; luxuriant, too, in vines and olives. Palms and prickly pear give to it a look of the Levant. In summer, the intense blue of the sky wearies the eyes. So does the pale dust and the bone-like pallor of limestone rock. Houses are a blinding white; roofs, golden. Its people have soft Arab eyes and an indolent Arab courtesy. They extend a more lavish welcome than in Castile but forget more quickly. They have much wit, less humour. They speak their Spanish with a lazy slur of syllables. They are lovers of laughter, but quickly moved to tears. They dance and sing, play the guitar, and array their donkeys with tassels and brightly-coloured harness. Their churches are darker than any I have seen, their Madonnas more lavishly decked with brocades and jewels and rings. Their Christs would move a heart of stone, yet have a primitive savagery like the carvings of ancient Mexico.

ELIZABETH HAMILTON *The Great Teresa*

VALENCIA

Es un paradiso habitado por demonios.
"It is a paradise occupied by devils."

Valencian saying

MURCIA

Cielo y suelo bueno, el entresuelo malo.
"A sky and soil that are good, while all between is indifferent."

Murcian saying

Ronda lies in the mountains of southern Andalusia. What more charming introduction could one have to Spain than the following, and what more typical of all that is most likable about the Spanish? Imagine the English in the same circumstances—or the Italians.

AN INTRODUCTION

It was, indeed, in following the habits of the sunlight at Ronda that I had my first contact with the simplicity and courtesy of the country Spaniard, and the doors of his country opened to me, as it were, by a charming gesture. All the world loves an artist at work. For one thing, he can be placed, and his business in the country understood, when that of the tourist bewilders the simple. The reserve of the Spaniard is never surly. He requires his own personal dignity, but he will invariably allow you yours. If he knows what will please you, and you are a well-behaved person, he will of his own accord open an entrance to the interests you seek in his country.

There were certain elderly gentlemen who took their morning walk within the public alameda. It was also my habit to write there, and after observation of the habits of trees and their shadows, to go at a certain hour to the fragrant dusk of a pergola heavy with roses and lilac blooms. Here the shade remained all morning, and here I was joined by the elderly group who sat gravely exchanging the small talk of the town.

It happened that one morning I was at work upon a poem, and the irregular appearance of the lines upon the page drew the attention of one of the gentleman to my occupation. He observed in an undertone to one of his friends that I was a poet.

27

The gentlemen looked around. From beneath the gentle shadow of trailing petals the Judas-trees in monarch's purple could be seen and the sunlight caressed the hollows of the Sierras. "A fit place for a poet to write!" said the gentleman with satisfaction.

"Very truly, a fit place!" agreed the others.

Every morning we exchanged our salutations, when one morning a younger man joined the group, preparing to sit upon the bench which I occupied. He was at once interrupted. "Do not sit upon that bench," prevented one of the gentlemen in an undertone; "you may disturb the rhythm." The young man glanced, raised his hat and seated himself elsewhere. He evidently considered it reasonable. And one evening when I was sitting on the edge of the gorge as the sun was going down an elderly man in a cloak in whom I recognized one of my morning group seated himself near me. My back was towards the mountains. The old gentleman rose and approached me. He removed his hat and entreated me to look round. All these things happening in the heavens and a poet sitting unobservant? I rose. He waved his arm to the splendours. Poet— sunset! Sunset—poet! The introduction was made. I directed my smiles and my appreciation to the sunset and my bows to my dignified old friend.

GERTRUDE BONE *Days in Old Spain*, 1938

Church and Palace,
Town and City

Lovers of architecture must prefer Spain to Italy. It is a different problem, altogether, where painting is concerned, but, with architecture, there can be no question of doubt; the Spaniards have been the greatest builders since the Romans.

SACHEVERELL SITWELL

It was a surprise, when I was in Madrid a few years ago, to find, almost completed, "the highest residential building in Europe". Not to mention, next to it and dwarfed by it, a twenty-five-storey hotel with a swimming pool on the top. From skyscrapers to Roman aqueducts, Gothic cathedrals to mediaeval cities, there are enough remarkable buildings in Spain to keep the most ambitious tourist hurrying. And for lovers of Baroque . . .

WITH ROME AND JERUSALEM

The most splendid building in Santiago de Compostela is the western façade of the cathedral, known as El Obradoiro. It consists of a huge central body in three parts, or it is, in fact, a centre piece with wings, standing on a ramp above a double external staircase that climbs in two flights, with a double row of balusters. This façade is in two storeys, flanked by Corinthian pillars, and forming a huge frame to hold up the statue of St James. It is an immense gable ending in a cupola, and having first a pair of niches and then one gigantic niche, that hold statues, increasing in size, of the patron saint. It spreads itself, with two lesser gables, across the base of the two towers, two hundred and thirty feet high, all in golden stone, and with snapdragons and other flowers growing in the interstices. The towers, up to their first storey, where they stand on a level with the topmost statue of St James, are faced with five Doric pilasters on each of their sides, and then climb in two diminishing storeys, ending in a balustrade of obelisks and a high cupola.

Seen from below, El Obradoiro is one of the most splendidly fantastic buildings in the world, and except that it is saner and cleanlier it speaks the ecstatic language of the Jain and Hindu temples and could shake its incense-shedding towers above the white-clad crowds and lily tanks at Madura. . . .

In its towering magnificence it transcends the years of decadence and must be numbered with the great buildings of the world. This remote corner of Spain, so famous as a shrine for pilgrims in the Middle Ages, is still to be ranked with Rome and with Jerusalem.

SACHEVERELL SITWELL *Spain*

No building in Spain has been more described than Philip II's convent-palace, the gloomy Escorial. Its setting is depressing enough, overhung by the grey rocks and pines of Sierra de Guadarrama. It is a building I do not like but cannot forget.

THE ESCORIAL

The whole building consists of a palace, a church, a convent, and a burial-place for the sovereigns of Spain. It was began in 1563, by Philip II in consequence of a vow he made, if he should vanquish the French army near St Quintin's, which he did in 1557, on St Laurence's day. The architects were John Bat. Monegro of Toledo, and John de Herrara, who finished it in 1586. It is dedicated to St Laurence: and as this saint is said to have been broiled alive on a gridiron, in the third century, the founder chose to have the building on the plan of that culinary instrument, the bars of which form several courts, and the handle the royal apartments.

Gridirons are met with in every part of this building; there are sculptured gridirons, painted gridirons, iron gridirons, wooden gridirons, and stucco gridirons: there are gridirons over the doors, gridirons in the yards, gridirons in the windows, gridirons in the galleries. Never was instrument of martyrdom so multiplied, so honoured, so celebrated: and thus much for gridirons. I never see a broiled beefsteak without thinking of the Escorial.

RICHARD TWISS *Travels through Portugal and Spain*, 1773

When I first saw Cordova it was of the North African town of Xauen that I was at once reminded, hardly surprising perhaps since Xauen, which lies in the Riff mountains of what used to be Spanish Morocco, was

built there by a Spanish Moor. Here, in Cordova, was
the same maze of tiny streets, the same white-washed
houses which seemed too small to live in, let alone be
used for shop and workshop in addition as some of
them are. Here in fact was the feel of an Arab medina,
not a town in Spain. At the heart of Cordova stands one
of the world's most astonishing buildings, once mosque,
now a church second only in size to St Peter's at Rome.

THE GREAT MOSQUE OF CORDOVA

To have seen the Mosque of Cordova forms an era in one's
life. It is so vast, so solemn, so beautiful. You seem to be
wandering at sunset time in a large and dusky forest, intersected
by regular alleys of tall, stately palms. No matter in what
direction you turn your face, northward, southward, eastward,
westward, the same beautiful perspective meets your eyes, file
after file of marble and jasper columns supporting the double
horse-shoe arch. Nothing can be more imposing, and at the
same time graceful, than this arrangement of transverse aisles;
and the interlaced arches, being delicately coloured in red and
white, may not inaptly be compared to foliage of a palm-forest,
flushed with the rays of the setting sun. If so impressive now,
what must this place have been in the glorious days of Abder-
rahman, the Al-Raschid of Cordova, when the roofs blazed
with arabesques of red and blue and "patines of bright gold";
the floors were covered with gorgeous carpets, and the aisles
swarmed with thousands of worshippers in their bright Eastern
dresses. The richest imagination cannot ever paint the scene,
the readiest fancy cannot embellish it, and only those who have
imbibed the rich colours of the East can close their eyes and
dream of it. When the dream is over, cast your eyes along the
long lines of columns, and you will see where the shoulders of
spectators and worshippers of ages have left an enduring mark—
a touching sight!—and then go into the once exquisite Maksura
or Caliph's seat, and weep to see what becomes of beautiful
things in Spain.

MATILDA BETHAM EDWARDS
Through Spain to the Sahara, 1868

How did it happen?

MOSQUE INTO CATHEDRAL

After the conquest of Cordova in 1236, St Ferdinand converted this mosque into a cathedral; and it preserved its

ancient plan until the time of Emperor Charles V. In the year 1528, the Spaniards began to disfigure its symmetry by modern erections, which continued to be made in succeeding reigns, in order to convert it more effectually into a temple for celebrating the solemn rites of the Christian religion; by which injudicious scheme both the Moorish and Christian architectures are deprived of every thing like unity of design. In vain have remonstrances been repeatedly made at different times, by the lovers of the arts, nay, even by royalty itself, against these misplaced and tasteless alterations. . . . Of this description is the choir, erected in the centre of the whole edifice; and which . . . were it in any other church, would deserve great praise for the Gothic grandeur of the plan, the loftiness of its dome, the exquisite carving of the stalls, and the elegance and high finishing of the arches and ornaments. But, placed as it is in the middle of the Arabian structure, it destroys all unity of design; darkens the rest; and renders confused every idea of the original general effect of the building.

Many are the chapels, erected in various parts between the pillars; which indeed form so many distinct churches in the midst of the old cathedral, interrupt the enfilade, and block up the passage. In one place, columns have been removed, in order to adorn these same chapels: in another, we are credibly informed, pieces of the beautiful timber-work, that supports the roof, have been taken away for the purpose of making musical instruments, especially guitars, for which use this kind of wood has been recommended, as being peculiarly proper!!!

J. C. MURPHY *The Arabian Antiquities of Spain,* 1815

I have had a warm feeling for Seville since my first evening there when I asked at a café, in halting Spanish, the way to the address of a friend who was spending the summer there. Quite soon all the waiters and several customers had closed in and were reading what I had written on the menu. They shook their heads and began several different arguments among themselves in which the name of the street recurred with varying degrees of incredulity.

A boy was sent to call someone who was an expert on Seville and would certainly know, a second boy was sent to say that at this time of the evening he would be somewhere else, a third went for someone who, now they had remembered him, all agreed was an even greater expert on Seville. Gradually an awful doubt took hold of me and I surreptitiously checked with my friend's letter. The word was not Alfafar but Alfalfa.

How could I tell them, when I had caused all this trouble? It wasn't till two hours later, still surrounded by café customers and by at least three experts on Seville, who were buying me drinks in turn, that I thought of the solution. Once more, but this time openly for all to see I produced my friend's letter —and with astonishment I saw my mistake.

They were amazed. They were delighted. I had the surprising feeling that for the last hour they had guessed and approved of the way I wasn't telling them. We went the five streets to my friend's lodgings in a sort of triumphal procession, since when I have always enjoyed with him a reputation for spontaneous international bonhomie.

But to more serious matters: Seville was hardly the place I expected to find the largest Gothic church in the world.

A MOUNTAIN IN A CITY

If you try to imagine St Paul's Cathedral in the centre of a town the size of Bradford, you have some idea of the disproportionate space occupied by Seville Cathedral. Miles away you see this Gothic pyramid rising from the plain, and when you are in Seville its bulk dominates all things. It is like having a mountain in the middle of a city, with little doors in it through which men pass in and out, as gnomes enter a hillside.

The guide-books call it the largest Gothic church in the world and the largest of any except St Peter's; but it is infinitely odder than that. In order to understand Seville Cathedral you should first see the mosque of Córdoba. More modest than Seville, Córdoba decided to build a cathedral inside the mosque and to leave the mosque standing round it, but in Seville they decided to demolish the mosque and cover with a Christian church the colossal area it had occupied. It is curious to think that the architects of Seville Cathedral were really Moslems, and that in spite of everything their mosque still shines through in the rectangular shape of this vast church.

When I entered the perpetual twilight of the cathedral, a poor little woman attached herself to me and fluttered shapelessly and noiselessly like a black bat, whining the Christian equivalent of "alms for the love of Allah"; and when I placed a trifle in her hand she blessed me and faded into the shadows. I stood amazed by the size of this church, not delighted and

33

impressed as one is in St Peter's, but overwhelmed by this immensity of gloom, by the colossal nave pillars rising to the cavernous vaulting. Upon the great expanse of floor a group of tourists, or a priest and his acolyte, looked like insects as they crawled across the pavement.

The side chapels, where Masses were being said, glowed like little jewellers' shops in some vast deserted market square; and when I came to the tomb of Columbus I saw four giant heralds, representing Castile, León, Aragon and Navarre, bearing upon their shoulders the coffin of the navigator; and these more than human-sized figures seemed, like everything else, out of scale.

But the Cathedral is full of exquisite things that shine and glitter. A great deal of South American gold, one imagines, still gleams upon the crowns of Virgins and the limbs of cupids, and the *retablo* behind the high altar seems to hold the population of a fair-sized medieval town; but to appreciate it you need either a step-ladder or a pair of field glasses.

Every year at Corpus Christi choristers in the dress of three centuries ago dance in front of this altar to the sound of castanets; and if I had to choose, I would rather see this dance of the Seises than the famous ceremonies of Holy Week. The boys wear satin knee-breeches, jackets hanging from one shoulder, buckled shoes, and plumed hats, and they perform a grave and stately measure. It is a unique survival of the religious dancing which was always popular in Spain, though the Church was more than a little doubtful about it. From what I have read of the Dance of the Seises, it is the last vestige of these ancient ballets. Even so, Rome was anxious to put a stop to it, and Pope Eugenius IV allowed the dance to continue, so the story goes, only as long as the costumes should last. It is said that, in order to keep up the custom, the dresses have been cunningly patched and re-patched until hardly a shred of the original garments remains.

H. V. MORTON *A Stranger in Spain*, 1955

Churches and monasteries have not been Spain's only remarkable buildings. What must have been the most splendid of all Spanish palaces was built before A.D. 1000. Sadly, it is now a ruin.

THE PALACE OF ZEHRA

Three miles from Cordoba, in honour of his favourite Sultana, the third and greatest of the Abderahmans constructed the city, palace and gardens of Zehra. Twenty-five years and above three millions sterling were employed by the founder: his liberal taste invited the artists of Constantinople, the most skilful sculptors and architects of the age, and the buildings were sustained and adorned by twelve hundred columns of Spanish and African, of Greek and Indian marble. The hall of audience was encrusted with gold and pearls, and a great basin in the centre was surrounded with the curious and costly figures of birds and quadrupeds. In a lofty pavilion of the gardens, one of these basins and fountains, so delightful in a sultry climate, was replenished not with water, but with the purest quicksilver. The seraglio of Abderahman, his wives, concubines and black eunuchs amounted to six thousand three hundred persons; and he was attended to the field by a guard of twelve thousand horse, whose belts and scimitars were studded with gold.

EDWARD GIBBON
The Decline and Fall of the Roman Empire

And of course, not to be left out, the palace-fortress of the Alhambra, a building for which I have to summon a little second-hand enthusiasm since I have only seen it in drenching rain.

A MOORISH PARADISE

The city of Granada lay in the centre of the kingdom, sheltered as it were in the lap of Sierra Nevada, or chain of snowy mountains. It covered two lofty hills, and a deep valley that divides them, through which flows the river Darro. One of these hills was crowned by the royal palace and fortress of the Alhambra, capable of containing forty thousand men within its walls and towers. There is a Moorish tradition, that the king who built this mighty pile was skilled in the occult sciences, and furnished himself with gold and silver for the purpose by means of alchymy. Certainly never was there an edifice accomplished in a superior style of barbaric magnificence; and the stranger who, even at the present day, wanders among its silent and deserted courts and ruined halls, gazes with astonishment at its gilded and fretted domes and luxurious decorations, still retaining their brilliancy and beauty, in defiance of the ravages of time.

Opposite to the hill on which stood the Alhambra was its rival hill, on the summit of which was a spacious plain, covered with houses, and crowded with inhabitants. It was commanded by a fortress called the Alcazaba. The declivities and skirts of these hills were covered with houses to the number of seventy thousand, separated by narrow streets and small squares, according to the custom of Moorish cities. The houses had interior courts and gardens, refreshed by fountains and running streams, and set out with oranges, citrons, and pomegranates; so that, as the edifices of the city rose above each other on the sides of the hill, they presented a mingled appearance of city and grove, delightful to the eye. The whole was surrounded by high walls, three leagues in circuit, with twelve gates, and fortified by a thousand towers. The elevation of the city, and the neighbourhood of the Sierra Nevada, crowned with perpetual snows, tempered the fervid rays of summer; and thus, while other cities were panting with the sultry and stifling heat of the dog-days, the most salubrious breezes played through the marble halls of Granada.

The glory of the city, however, was its vega, or plain, which spread out to a circumference of thirty-seven leagues, surrounded by lofty mountains. It was a vast garden of delight, refreshed by numerous fountains, and by the silver windings of the Xenil. The labour and ingenuity of the Moors had diverted the waters of this river into thousands of rills and streams and diffused them over the whole surface of the plain. Indeed they had wrought up this happy region to a degree of wonderful prosperity, and took a pride in decorating it, as if it had been a favourite mistress. The hills were clothed with orchards and vineyards, the valleys embroidered with gardens, and the wide plains covered with waving grain. Here were seen in profusion the orange, the citron, the fig and pomegranate, with large plantations of mulberry trees, from which was produced the finest of silk. The vine clambered from tree to tree, the grapes hung in rich clusters about the peasant's cottage, and the groves were rejoiced by the perpetual song of the nightingale. In a word, so beautiful was the earth, so pure the air, and so serene the sky of this delicious region, that the Moors imagined the paradise of their prophet to be situate in that part of the heaven which overhung the kingdom of Granada.

WASHINGTON IRVING *The Conquest of Granada*, 1829

It is in her domestic palaces, even better perhaps than in her great public buildings, that Spain's history can be traced.

A LITTLE CORNER OF FRANCE BESIDE THE TAGUS

Aranjuez is a miracle. Thirty miles south of Madrid it is a green oasis on the River Tagus. Everywhere else in New Castile is dry, yellow and parched. But in Aranjuez, there are green lawns, fountains, light breezes, and in summer its famous strawberries seem huge and rich like lotus fruit. It was the natural place for the Spanish monarchs to have their summer palace as they had, with little interruption, since the late fifteenth century, when the mediaeval owners of the town, the knightly order of the Masters of Santiago, handed it over, reluctantly, to the Catholic kings Ferdinand and Isabella. The existing Royal Palace was built in the mid-eighteenth century by Philip V and his son Ferdinand VI, partly at least in imitation of their French cousins' magnificence at Versailles. And at the bottom of the royal gardens, along the Tagus, there is the Casita del Labrador, the neo-classical "Labourer's Cottage" built for Charles IV and Maria Luisa, those two strange rulers whose fantastic faces stare out forever, with their children, from their brilliantly insulting portraits by Goya.

The Casita del Labrador was no doubt built with the conscious recollection of Trianon at Versailles in the mind of the architect, Isidro González Velázquez, who worked on the house between 1792 and 1803. The site chosen was that of a real labourer's cottage, some of whose foundations are still visible in the cellars of the present house. This is built in the form of a three-storeyed central block, with two wings, themselves divided by a courtyard and united at their extremity by railings. The courtyard, as customary in neo-classical buildings of this type, is surrounded by twenty marble busts and statues, all being copies of a classic model, most being Roman emperors. These stand out against the pink and white brick of the Casita del Labrador itself, and the lush green of the woods which closely approach the house.

Inside, the principal and first floor is now alone properly maintained. This is reached by means of a sumptuous principal staircase, with marble steps and lined jade pillars. This leads to a suite of eighteen rooms whose principal characteristic is the collection of tapestries from the Fábrica del Buen Retiro, of furniture and, among other *objects d'art*, of clocks ("How can I be expected to rule an empire," complained the idiotic and displeasing monarch Ferdinand VII, prowling about these marble rooms, "when I cannot get all my clocks to keep the right time?"). The most splendid rooms are those associated with Queen Maria Luisa, in particular her drawing-room with its magnificent tapestry and the fine baroque ceiling of the four seasons painted by the Valencian artist, Maella. A specially curious clock here is decorated by a representation of Copernicus' planetary system. Four fine Sèvres bowls recall a gift to Maria Luisa by Napoleon. This room leads into the superb *Gabinete de Platino*, a room heavily encrusted with gold, bronze and platinum, carried out with much "Pompeian" imitations— as was inevitable at that period in the development of European

37

taste. (There is one entire Pompeian room, full of copies of Roman heads.) The walls are additionally adorned by small views of Italian cities: Florence, Venice, Naples; while from the ceiling hangs a great chandelier, a present of Pope Gregory XVI to Ferdinand VII. Opening off this splendid piece of extravagance, there is the royal bathroom, also lavishly decorated in a Pompeian style, but never alas used: for there do not seem to have been any occasions when the Royal Family every stayed the night at the Casita del Labrador. They only used it as a kind of adult day-nursery, where Maria Luisa might meet her absurd Godoy, the Prince of Peace, in slightly less formal circumstances than was inevitable at the big palace nearer the town.

The most touching part of this jewelled house is perhaps the elegant but severely functional service staircase. On its walls, the painter Zacarias González Velázquez (brother of the architect) has depicted a brilliant series of dancing portraits, one of his own son, another of Maria Luisa's hair-dresser, a third of Charles IV's barber. Other servants follow, half erased by time, but full of movement, gaiety and gravity, lasting expressions of that other Spain so rich in character but so little understood by the cold, mad, royal persons upstairs whom they had to serve

HUGH THOMAS *Great Houses of Europe*, 1961

Everyone will have his favourite Spanish town, and mine is Avila—perhaps because, unlike almost every other town I know, it is a complete thing and not a formless straggle, spreading over the countryside. Or perhaps because its astonishing walls make it possible to imagine the life of a mediaeval town in a way in which no history book can.

AVILA

Avila is the only completely walled medieval city in Europe. The walls have eighty-six towers and the only way to get in or out of the city is by one of the nine gates. When you look at Avila from the road to Salamanca, which I think is the best of all the views, the town, a narrow oblong in shape, is tilted slightly towards you. You can see the mass of red-tiled roofs inside the walls, lying at various angles, and the tallest building of all, the cathedral, is not in the centre of the city, as you might expect, but forms an immense bastion in the eastern angle of the wall. You notice too that quite an area in the western part of Avila is waste and uninhabited, for the population within the walls in the Middle Ages was greater than it is now. One day while I was admiring this truly exquisite relic of the medieval world, a Spaniard on his way to Salamanca stopped his car and joined me. "Ah," he said, "but you must come back in winter-time and see Avila in the snow. Then she is most beautiful."

I shall never forget my arrival by moonlight that first night. I soon left the shabby hotel and was roaming about looking for somewhere to dine. Near the cathedral was a plump little policeman wearing the usual white helmet, and to him I went asking advice. He could not have been more helpful or courteous, and he had such a friendly face that when I thanked him and called him señor, I lifted my hat on the impulse of the moment, before I turned away. To my utter astonishment, not to be outdone in manners, and maybe considering a salute too officious, he lifted his white helmet several inches from his head as if it had been a bowler hat, at the same time bowing deeply. This put me in a good humour for several days and I often smiled to remember it.

H. V. MORTON *A Stranger in Spain*

People, no doubt, get the towns they deserve; Barcelona, capital of the Catalonians, is certainly not the most beautiful in Spain, but it is probably the most lively and entertaining. When I was last there it was, among other things, the smelliest, and the one where I saw the most exciting dancing.

BARCELONA

Barcelona is the focus and centre of Catalanism, in all its proud, turbulent independence. More, perhaps than any city in the world (Marseilles and Naples are near rivals) it gives an impression of tempestuous, surging, irrepressible life and *brio*. A Barcelona crowd roused to anger would be intimidating in a high degree. It is even a little intimidating when in its usual good humour. Drivers charge about the narrow streets and broad squares, sounding their horns loudly and continuously for sheer joy of noise; trams crash along, jangling shrill bells. After Barcelona, Madrid seems a genteel and almost soundless city. The Barcelonese seem to shout, scream, blow horns, laugh, stare, crowd, chatter, hang out flags, all day and all night. Up and down the Ramblas they walk and talk, buy and sell, drink in cafés, stare with unflagging interest at passers by (their preoccupation with people is as intense as elsewhere in Spain; never for a moment do they seem to neglect the proper study of mankind—only for "man" one should substitute "woman").

39

The famous Ramblas are delightful; divided by a shady grove of plane trees, two narrow one-way streets run north and south, through the length of the Old Town, crowded with cafés, shops, kiosks, people, trams, motor vehicles, boot-blacks and sellers of lottery tickets. On the dividing promenade people stroll, among brilliant flower stalls, newspaper kiosks, *estanquillos*, and stalls crowded with birds in cages—parakeets, pigeons, blue, green and yellow tits, who fill the air with their liquid twitterings. Beside them swim goldfish, crabs and water tortoises; white mice, guinea-pigs, little dogs, and tiny chimpanzees run to and fro in their boxes, and all is animation. Secretive youths sidle up; insinuatingly they try to persuade you to buy a watch, or a fountain pen, or a ring, for three hundred pesetas; they come quickly down to thirty, twenty, ten; they end by seeming to beg you to take it as a gift, as if the police were (as perhaps they are) hot on their tracks. Buxom women and girls, with fine hatless heads of black hair, smart men with white suits and dark glasses and canes, nippy street urchins, assiduous persons offering lottery tickets—they might, no doubt, be met with in any Spanish town, but here they seem to wear a peculiar air of confidence and vivacity. I do not think they sleep, or even go to bed. My bedroom overlooked the Rambla; when, soon after midnight, I went to bed, the population were always still strolling down there in a high state of animation. One morning I was awakened at four by loud conversation; going out on to my balcony and looking down, I perceived that the Rambla was still full of people sitting at café tables or on seats beneath the trees, or strolling to and fro, talking, laughing and screaming with the greatest vivacity, the street lights that gleamed above the plane trees now paling a little in a faint dawn. I dare say the flower stalls and the bird and animal stalls and the little boot-shiners were all there too. It was a pretty and fantastic sight, this crowd bewitched into perpetual nocturnal animation.

The Barcelonese are, indeed, a vivid and a tireless people: one sees why they have always had so many revolutions, bombs, commotions, aspirations, political movements, industries and wealth. Their spirit and energy are tremendous. Directly General Franco began his revolution, the Barcelona incendiaries rushed jubilantly round their churches and set them on fire. Church-burning, which has been called the second national sport of Spain, has nearly always been part of Spanish revolutions; the hatred of church and priests has bitten so deep into a large proportion of this religious people that churches are burnt down and priests are murdered; when the revolutionary side is pro-clerical, this gesture has to be made by the loyalists. The first attack on church and religious orders was in Queen Christina's days; the last Barcelona large-scale church burnings had been in July 1909, when sixty-three religious buildings had been attacked. Those riots began as an expression of distaste (somewhat irrelevant) for the war in Morocco. . . . But in July, 1936, after the rising of the army, the Barcelona mobs got down to it in earnest, and nearly all the convents and churches were lit; only the modern Sagrada Familia and the Cathedral (which was later hit by nationalist bombs) escaped altogether. Fortunately Catalonian churches are solidly built; in most cases, even when the interiors were burnt out, the external structure proved less inflammable and, though the incendiaries did what they could during that reign of savagery and terror, when human lives and human art alike became a holocaust to mob passion and brutality, few buildings were destroyed past repair. Others have been well and quickly restored. On the whole Barcelona, ten years after the war, has not the appearance of a city badly scarred, either from fire or from bombs.

ROSE MACAULAY *Fabled Shore*, 1949

Anthony Carson's misadventures in Granada, make mine seem small, but it was exasperating at the time when I came for the plane to be told that it now flew not on Mondays, Wednesdays and Fridays but on Tuesdays, Thursdays and Saturdays. There is nothing like being compelled to stay in a place, however beautiful and full of historic interest, for giving you a grudge against it; in that twenty-four hours I remember, among other things, seeing more stray dogs run down by big rich cars which didn't stop than in any similar period before or since.

A VISIT TO GRANADA

In Granada I stayed in a pension directly opposite the Bodega Munoz. Every day I intended to leave Granada for the north, for Paris, for England, for all that was overdue, looming, side-stepped. But there, right opposite my front door, was the Bodega Munoz. It was a cruel piece of town-planning. A pause on the front-door step, a long precise glance at my watch, a moment of feigned despair, a tiny voice to be stifled, and then in. Into the deep, cool, sherry-laden gloom, where the fat wine barrels winked at you like merry monks, and the glasses chinked and the world was lost in a buzz of talk. Stand still in Granada and you will find a friend. You need not order a drink. A glass is put into your hand.

After the Bodega Munoz there was always the Alhambra

41

and the Generalife. Somebody would say: "You must come and
see our Alhambra." Or there was a new tourist girl at the
pension who would say: "I am just dying to see the Alhambra. . . ." I would never be a fit guide to explain the architectural
details of this place: directly I arrived at the Patio of the
Fountains, I fell asleep, lulled by nightingales and gurgling
water. When I woke up, guide or girl was gone. That girl would
be inevitably picked up in the Patio of the Lions because
foreign-girl-hunting is an established minor industry in Granada,
with its headquarters in the Alhambra.

Few natives of Granada otherwise visit it, except on Sundays
when entrance is free, and everybody goes, angrily and
stridently, just to show whom it belongs to. Outside the
Alhambra is an unpretentious rustic café, where the foreign-
girl-hunters post their spies. You can buy good, cheap manzanilla here and drowse under the tall trees; there is a slight
odour of sanctity. Spaniards give little thought to animals, but
outside the Alhambra great respect is shown to civilisation.
One of my guides once jumped up in a fury and shouted at a
boy who was thrashing a donkey. "Barbarian," he yelled.
"Haven't you enough culture to refrain from beating donkeys
here?"

The only trouble with the Bodega Munoz was the difficulty
in obtaining cigarettes, or, for that matter, obtaining them
anywhere in Granada. Rival cigarette gangs bought up all
available stocks and sold them in the streets for a profit. This
meant walking up and down Granada making signs at people
until one of them whipped out a packet. During one of these
sorties, between returning from the Alhambra and visiting the
Bodega, I suddenly decided to return to England. I walked
briskly into an agency to buy a ticket.

"No train, señor," said the clerk; "not until the day after
tomorrow."

I drifted back to the Bodega, and a glass was put into my
hand. My host was an elderly man with a sharp nose and a
bright eye. "Alas," he said, "you are seeing a dying Granada,
my friend. The spark has gone out of it. I suppose you would
like to visit the Alhambra? I would be delighted to accompany
you." I explained that I had just returned from sleeping in the
Patio of the Fountains. "To sleep is best," said my friend. "It
is really only an exquisite shell." He handed me his card. On it
was printed "Francisco Lorca."

"But are you related to the poet?" I asked.

The elderly man put his finger to his lips. "Please do not
discuss this matter here," he said. "Let us go somewhere
else."

I followed him out of the Bodega Munoz along a number of

streets and into a small bar. "Here we can talk freely," he said. "Tell me, do you know about Garcia Lorca?"

"Certainly," I replied. "His poetry is greatly loved in England, even in our translations."

"I am of his family. I saw him before he was murdered. He came from Madrid in June, 1936, to have a holiday in the family house in the Callejon del Nevot. The police called for him a month later. He was shot on the twenty-fourth of July and buried in the cemetery. He was the third member of our family to be murdered by the Fascist dogs. Twice I myself have hid on the roof. Granada is dead. There is no heart here. Dereliction, tourists and ruins."

"But can't one mention Garcia's name here?" I asked.

"By no means. His poetry can't be published. He doesn't exist. I don't exist." He swallowed his drink. "Would you care to hear some funny stories about the Generalissimo?" He told me some stories, including a very crude one about Gibraltar. Then he proposed that we visit the gypsies.

We walked up to the caves, speared by the professional cries of children. There was a slight derelict barrier of hate. "May the Glory of God descend on your beautiful face and give you a long life and countless children. Give me twenty pesetas." We entered a neat, white cave, and I met a family of twenty gypsies. They had everything that has been lost, that many don't know about, that some are always looking for. Happiness in the wrist, love in the eye, fire in the dress. A boy and a girl danced in and out of death without getting scathed. It was secure. A moon hung in the sky outside the cave and they danced there like flames, and squabbled. Then forty-five Germans arrived with cine-cameras and jokes, and the children came out of the caves with knives in their eyes and whined. My companion and I went back to the Bodega.

I intended to leave by the next available train, but a French girl arrived at the pension and was put at my table. "Je suis venue," she said, "pour voir l'Alhambra." I lost her in the Patio of the Lions, woke up and returned to the Bodega. Here somebody introduced me to a well-dressed middle-aged man who had the air of a permanent official, of someone who would always be just on the right side. He looked at me attentively and said little. His eyes were never off me for a second.

"This gentleman is a civil officer of the Falange," said a voice.

The Falangista examined me even more keenly and eventually spoke. "You are English?"

"Yes," I said.

"A tourist?"

"I don't know if that is the word. I used to live in Seville. I am a writer."

43

"Ah," said the Falangista with a lot of meaning in his voice.

I began to feel uncomfortable. But we continued drinking, and suddenly a ridiculous devil tapped me gently behind the ear.

"What do you think of Lorca?" I asked him.

He didn't reply, just gazed at me and flicked the ash off his cigarette. "Will you follow me outside?" he said suddenly.

"Certainly," I replied. I suddenly felt alone and small in the middle of Granada, as I followed the plump good-looking official through the streets.

"Where are we going?" I asked him, feeling in my pocket to make sure I had my passport.

"To Headquarters," he said shortly. "That building over there." He pointed to a grey, ominous building like a disguised prison. "Come inside," he said, holding open the door and leading me into a long room with an enormous counter. "What will you have? All drinks are free here." I ordered a manzanilla. "To the Queen of England," said the Falangista, holding up his glass. "You just asked me about Lorca, the magnificent poet of Granada. Ah Lorca. . . ." He started to recite: "*Verde, que te quiero verde*," paused for a moment trying to remember a word, when a small dark waiter leant across the bar counter and concluded the poem. "Lorca," said the waiter, pouring out more drinks, "was murdered by the Fascist dogs. Granada is dead and without heart."

"What do you think of our country?" asked the Falange official.

"Speak out," cried the waiter; "you are safe here."

I drank more manzanilla, summoning words. Spain was a dusty, broken country of buried talent. It was a country, like a ragged child undrained of gaiety, to love. I tried to say this through the manzanilla. Then there were more drinks, and the Falange official and the waiter told stories about the Generalissimo, recited another poem of Lorca, and told another, still cruder story about Gibraltar. "I must go to work," said the Falangista. I could see he was rather drunk, and he looked like all fairly successful men, the ones who dress well and cope with their superiors, who get drunk in Paris or London. He staggered out of the door and waved.

The next day I actually took the train to Valencia. Five minutes after we started, there was a terrible grinding noise and we waited for about an hour in a deluge of rain. Then we returned to Granada. The engine had broken down. The next train would be the day after tomorrow. I returned to the pension and sat down in the dining-room. At my table there was a pretty girl in a pink dress. "*Domani*," she said, over the fish, "*voglio andare all'Alhambra. . . .*"

Looking for a Bandit, 1961

Love, Courtship and Marriage

Hoy casado, mañana cansado.
"Married today, tired tomorrow."

Castilian saying

It was customary, until the nineteenth century, for a would-be suitor to announce his intentions by firing a rifle at his beloved's feet, usually when she was on her way home after Mass. She was expected not to turn a hair but to walk on with her eyes demurely cast upon the ground.

NINA EPTON

Nothing about the Spanish has seemed more strange to outsiders than their customs of love, courtship and marriage. I wish I could say that I had seen Valencians shooting at their girls' legs, or even cloaked Andalusians paying court at street windows. If today only the powerful metal grilles remain, and Spanish unmarried girls even go for rides on the pillions of motor scooters, these half oriental customs are not long dead and certainly flourished till the Civil War.

Better still to have actually *been* a Spanish *novio* attending his *novia* at her *reja*—as Gerald Brenan was.

CARMEN

Once in the late twenties I was staying at a small pension at Almeria, and feeling, as I often did in that beautiful city, a little bored, I decided to go for a walk. Returning through dusty lanes an hour or two later, at that disturbing hour when the sky above turns crimson and the whole street seems to be melting and dissolving in the dusk, I became aware of a pair of dark eyes looking at me through the bars of a window. I made a circle and walked past again. The eyes were still there, a pale Byzantine nose and mouth appeared beneath them, a smile drifted over them, and after another turn or two I found myself fixed to the spot and even holding on to the *reja*. The girl was called Carmen, and before I knew what had happened I was her *novio*.

My hours of duty were from seven to nine-thirty and from ten to twelve. I gulped down my dinner and had to cut out my usual coffee. There she would be, framed against the darkness of the room behind her but with the lights of the street catching her face, and a sweet but rather formal smile stamped on it. And then I would take up once again the task of making conversation through the bars of a window with a girl to whom I had absolutely nothing to say.

As a person Carmen did not make a clear impression on me, because her feelings were always masked by the role she was playing. In much of what she said she seemed to be carrying out a ritual. I never, for example, arrived at her window without her exclaiming, "How late you are!" or left without her asking, "Why are you in such a hurry to leave?" These phrases and many others seemed to be part of the formal language of *novio*-ship: we were playing at being lovers just as people when they paid an official call played at conversation. And finally when, at the stroke of twelve, half-dropping with fatigue, I tore myself away, she would smile and say in what was, I suppose, meant to be a roguish tone, "Now, mind you don't go off to one of those naughty places." It seemed as though the convention required that I should have been so worked up by these hours of *tête-à-tête* at the *reja* that I should be unable to resist that sort of vicarious satisfaction. . . .

My *noviazgo* came to an end in an abrupt and painful manner. I had been courting Carmen patiently and with circumspection for a couple of weeks and had got to the point where I was allowed to hold one of her fingers in my hand, when the crude Anglo-Saxon idea came to me that it was time to take another step forward and give her a kiss through the bars of the cage. But when I attempted to do this there was an immediate reaction. Drawing back several feet into the room she declared, though with a smile to soften the harshness of her refusal, that no man's lips had ever touched hers nor would they be allowed to do so until her husband bestowed his on her upon their bridal night. Then, seeing that these words had a chilling effect upon me, she made an offer. She would meet me on the following afternoon at a certain place in the public gardens accompanied by her young sister, and we would walk up and down a little. Only I must understand that this was an extraordinary concession which she would never have agreed to if I had not been a foreigner, accustomed to greater freedom than Spaniards in these matters.

The hour came and I approached the rendezvous. And there,

at the end of the alley, I saw two girls dressed in black shiny silk, standing with their hands folded in front of them under a white-flowered trumpet tree. One of them was young, a mere child, while the other, who might have been twenty-four, was short and squat, almost a dwarf. She had the face of Carmen—it was a handsome and distinguished face and by no means a stupid one—but oh, that body! In an access of panic I turned and fled, unable to face the ordeal of meeting her and pretending that nothing had happened, when in fact her shortness had made my tallness seem a deformity.

After this the situation was naturally beyond explanation. That night I had several drinks before I could summon up the courage to confront her at her window. As I came up to it I could see her strongly boned white face and dark, heavily arched eyes looking out through the bars. She had not changed out of her unbecoming black dress, but her lips were more thickly made up than ever and she had put a red lily in place of a carnation in her hair. There was a stronger smell than usual of jasmine water, and she seemed, I could not exactly see how, to have grown tall and slim again. Hurriedly I gave her the box of chocolates I had bought and, without mentioning my failure in the afternoon, told her that I had had a telegram saying that my mother was ill and that I was leaving next morning for England. She offered her condolences—pretending was what she was good at—and I promised to write. Gently and as if believing me, she smiled. But that facial cast, severe and melancholy as of a lady-in-waiting at the court of the Paleologues, did not exist for nothing, and I knew that she was proud and incredulous underneath. Then I said goodbye. As I bent to kiss her hand a door opened behind letting in some light and I saw that she was standing on a low wooden platform. No, I had not been mistaken.

For some *novios*, circumstances were still more uncomfortable.

GATERAS—CAT DOORS

In the street doors of most old houses in Spanish cities there is or used to be a small hole cut close to the ground for the use of cats. . . . These *gateras*, as they were called, were in some districts used by *novios* in the place of windows. The man lay or crouched on the pavement or cobbles, and the girl took up a similar position inside, but—this was the point of the arrangement—invisible to passers-by and thus protected from glances which might have hurt her modesty. I have seen this method

47

of courtship in use in the Albaicín of Granada, but its real home was in certain large pueblos of the provinces of Cadiz and Seville, where old-fashioned habits lingered late. Here on any night of the year one could see in one of those long, empty streets of the country towns, dazzlingly white by moonlight, a row of cloaked and prostrate figures discoursing in whispers to their *novias* within.

GERALD BRENAN South from Granada, 1957

At one time it was a serious problem of house planning in Spain that no family with teenage daughters would live in an upstairs flat, thus losing any chance of marrying them off.

BALEARIC COURTING

It seems strange that the courting should be transacted from the pavement in a town where the houses are as high as Palma, and where the upper storeys only are inhabited. The tender confidences are, of necessity, not whispered but shouted at the pitch of the voice so that the passer-by is entertained during his monotonous walk. The more bashful ones in Palma, however, hit upon a happy expedient. The lady at her window in the upper storey, or the maid for her benefit, bores a hole at the end of the water-pipe; the gentleman bores a hole at his end, nearer the pavement, and with the assistance of this telephone . . . the conversation is transmitted direct to the one ear for which it is intended.

When we crossed over to Mahón in Minorca we particularly admired the patience of the lovers in that quiet little town and congratulated them when we found that the ground-floor was inhabited instead of the upper, as unfortunately in Palma. At Mahón the lady sits in the room with her mantilla becomingly arranged and a red rose in her hair, the outspread fan helping the expression of her thoughts, while above it her black eyes flash now defiantly now tenderly at the lover who stands on the pavement with the green shutters sometimes drawn round him, the windows here being made English fashion *à la guillotine*, as though on purpose to decapitate clandestine lovers, so that his legs remain visible—usually, I noticed, cased in uniform with a scarlet stripe. In the middle of the day, when everyone else is enjoying the siesta, the stranger may perceive several pairs of legs adding colour to the dim perspective of the street while waiting for the "upper storey" to allow them to proceed.

GRAHAM BELLINGHAM, 1883

HIS CIGAR

*In Victorian times a Spaniard was never without a cigar in his mouth
"sleep, not bed, time only excepted". And it is still no status symbol.
A workman in overalls will finish his meal with a cigar and black
coffee while he painfully spells out his newspaper word by word*

IN A DRY LAND

Of all the Roman remains in Spain the aqueduct at Segovia is the most impressive, not only for its size and length but because it goes from hillside to hillside across one of the town's main plazas

THE ALCAZAR

Rebuilt in Gothic style after being burned down in 1862, and restored after a second destruction in the Civil War, this originally Moorish fortress guards the western extremity of the ancient hill-top town of Segovia

THE GREAT MOSQUE
OF CORDOBA

*Its columns are more like trees than masonry.
Wandering among them you seem to
be in a fantastic red and white forest*

During the War of the Spanish Succession an English expeditionary force captured Barcelona and fought a number of other remarkably successful, forgotten battles in eastern Spain. With them was a Captain George Carleton whose memoirs of the campaign and of the three years he spent as a well-treated prisoner of the Spanish are full of vivid observation—as well as decent protestant sentiment. As with most occupying armies, fraternization caused problems.

DEEPER SEAS

Valencia is famous for fine women. It indeed abounds in them; and among those, are great numbers of courtezans, not inferior in beauty to any. Nevertheless, two of our English officers, not caring for the common road, however safe, resolved to launch into the deeper seas, though attended with much greater danger. Amours, the common failing of that fair city, was the occasion of this accident, and two nuns the objects. It is customary in that country for young people to resort to the grates of the nunneries, there to divert themselves, and the nuns, with a little pleasant and inoffensive chit-chat. . . .

Our two officers were very assiduous at the grates of a nunnery in this place; and, having there pitched upon two nuns, prosecuted their amours with such vigour, that, in a little time, they had made a very great progress in their affections, without in the least considering the dangers that must attend themselves and the fair; they had exchanged vows, and prevailed upon the weaker vessels to endeavour to get out to their lovers. To effect which, soon after, a plot was laid; the means, the hour, and every thing agreed upon.

It is the custom of that nunnery, as of many others, for the nuns to take their weekly courses in keeping the keys of all the doors. The two love-sick ladies giving notice to their lovers at the grate, that one of their turns was come, the night and hour was appointed, which the officers punctually observing, carried off their prey without either difficulty or interruption.

But next morning when the nuns were missing, what an uproar was there over all the city! The ladies were both of quality; and therefore the tidings were first carried to their relations. They received the news with vows of utmost vengeance; and, as is usual in that country, put themselves in arms for that purpose. There needed no great canvassing for discovering who were the aggressors: the officers had been too frequent and too public in their addresses, to leave any room

49

for question. Accordingly they were complained of and sought for; but sensible at last of their past temerity, they endeavoured, and with a great deal of difficulty perfected, their escape.

Less fortunate were the two fair nuns; their lovers, in their utmost exigency, had forsaken them; and they, poor creatures, knew not where to fly. Under this sad dilemma they were taken; and, as in like offences, condemned directly to the punishment of immuring. And what greater punishment is there on earth, than to be confined between four narrow walls, only open at the top; and thence to be half supported with bread and water, till the offenders gradually starve to death?

The Earl of Peterborow, though highly exasperated at the proceedings of his officers, in compassion to the unhappy fair, resolved to interpose by all moderate means possible. He knew very well, that no one thing could so much prejudice the Spaniard against him, as the countenancing of such action; wherefore, he inveighed against the officers, at the same time that he endeavoured to mitigate in favour of the ladies; but all was in vain. . . . And, which was the hardest of all, the nearest of their relations most opposed all his generous mediations; and those, who, according to the common course of nature, should have thanked him for his endeavours to be instrumental in rescuing them from the impending danger, grew more and more enraged, because he opposed them in their design of a cruel revenge.

Notwithstanding all which, the earl persevered; and after a deal of labour, first got the penalty suspended; and, soon after, by the dint of a very considerable sum of money, (a most powerful argument, which prevails in every country,) saved the poor nuns from immuring; and at last, though with great reluctance, he got them received again into the nunnery. As to the warlike lovers, one of them was the year after slain at the battle of Almanza; the other is yet living, being a brigadier in the army.

CAPTAIN GEORGE CARLETON Memoirs

Henry Swinburne, an eighteenth-century traveller, observed the habits of the common people.

LAST FAVOURS

Our pleasurable ideas were a little ruffled by the sight of some hundreds of women in the villages, sitting in the sun lousing each other, or their husbands and children. When a young woman condescends to seek for lice in a man's head, it is supposed that the last favours have been granted by the fair one, or at least that he may have them for asking.

Travels through Spain, 1779

English and Spanish Royal Families have been involved in more than a few matrimonial skirmishes. An early episode in the life of Charles I is not so well remembered as his later execution by parliament, but at the time the highly unpopular plan of his father, James I, to marry him to the king of Spain's daughter was a nine-day wonder, not least because of the way he went about it. For on March 7th 1623 Prince Charles arrived in Marid to woo the infanta Doña María in person. He had ridden across France incognito with the Duke of Buckingham, under the original names of John Brown and Tom Smith.

THE SPANISH MATCH

The great business of the match was tending to a period . . . and there wanted nothing to consummate all things, when to the wonderment of the World, the Prince and the Marquis of Buckingham, arrived at this Court on Friday last upon the close of the evening: They alighted at my Lord of Bristol's House and the Marquis (Mr Thomas Smith), came in first with a portmanteau under his arm; then the Prince (Mr John Brown) was sent for, who stay'd awhile on t'other side of the street in the dark. My Lord of Bristol, in a kind of astonishment, brought him up to his bedchamber, where he presently called for Pen and Ink, and dispatched a Post that night to England, to acquaint His Majesty, how in less than sixteen days he was come to the Court of Spain; that Post went lightly laden, for he carried but three letters. The next day came Sir Francis Cottington and Mr Porter, and dark rumours ran in every corner how some great man was come from England; and some would not stick to say among the vulgar it was the king: but towards evening on Saturday, the Marquis went in a close coach to Court, where he had private Audience of this King, who sent Olivares to accompany him back to the Prince, where he kneeled and kissed his hands and hugged his thighs, and delivered how immeasurably glad his Catholick Majesty was of his coming, with other high compliments, which Mr Porter did interpret. About ten a clock that night the King himself came in a close carriage with intent to visit the Prince, who hearing of it, met him half-way; and after salutations and divers embraces which passed in the first interview, they parted

51

late. . . . On Sunday following the King in the Afternoon came abroad to take the air with the Queen, his two brothers and the Infanta, who were all in one coach; but the Infanta sat in the Boot with a blue ribbon about her arm of purpose that the Prince might distinguish her. And now it was quickly known among the vulgar that it was the Prince of Wales who was come. . . . As soon as the Infanta saw the Prince her colour rose very high, which we hold to be an impression of Love and Affection. . . .

There are many excellent Poems made here since the Prince's arrival. . . . I will venture to send you this one stanza of Lope de Vega's:—

Carlos Estuardo Soy	"I am Charles Stuart
Que siendo Amor *mi guia,*	And as love is my guide
Al cielo d'España voy	I go to the Spanish sky
Por ver mi Estrella Maria.	To see my star Maria."

There are comedians once a week come to the Palace, where under a great Canopy the Queen and the Infanta sit in the middle, our prince and Don Carlos on the Queen's right hand. I have seen the Prince have his eyes immoveably fixed upon the Infanta half an hour together in a thoughtful speculative posture which sure would needs be tedious, unless affection did sweeten it: it was no handsome comparison of Olivares that he watched her as a cat doth a mouse. Not long since the Prince, understanding that the Infanta was used to go some mornings to the *Casa de Campo,* a summer house the King hath on t'other side the River, to gather Maydew, he rose betimes and went thither, taking Mr Porter with him; they were let into the House and into the Garden, but the Infanta was in the Orchard: and there being a high partition wall between, and the door doubly bolted, the Prince got on the top of the wall and sprang down a great height, and so made towards her; but she spying him first of all the rest, gave a shriek and ran back: the old Marquis that was then her Guardian, came towards the Prince, and fell on his knees, conjuring His Highness to retire, in regard he hazarded his Head if he admitted any to her company; so the door was opened and he came out under that wall over which he had got in. I have seen him watch a long hour together in a close coach in the open street, to see her as she went abroad: I cannot say that the Prince did ever talk with her privately, yet publickly often, my Lord of Bristol being Interpreter; but the King always sat hard by to overhear all.

JAMES HOWELL *Letter to Sir Thomas Savage,* 1623

Flirtation with the eyes, another Spanish speciality, has an ancient history.

OF HINTING WITH THE EYES

After verbal allusion, when once the lover's advance has been accepted and an accord established, the next step consists in hinting with the glances of the eyes. Glances play an honourable part in this phase, and achieve remarkable results. . . .

To make a signal with the corner of the eye is to forbid the lover something; to droop the eye is an indication of consent; to prolong the gaze is a sign of suffering and distress; to break off the gaze is a mark of relief; to make signs of closing the eyes is an indicated threat. To turn the pupil of the eye in a certain direction and then to turn it back swiftly, calls attention to the presence of a person so indicated. A clandestine signal with the corner of both eyes is a question; to turn the pupil rapidly from the middle of the eye to the interior angle is a demonstration of refusal; to flutter the pupils of both eyes this way and that is a general prohibition. The rest of these signals can only be understood by actually seeing them demonstrated.

IBN HAZM (994–1064) *The Ring of the Dove*

The Spanish may still have a half-Moorish attitude to their women, but in no country did the mediaeval tradition of knights and maidens flourish and reach such absurdities as it did in Spain. Cervantes' Don Quixote was in part a satire on Amadis of Gaul, the greatest of Spanish knights of fiction.

DON QUIXOTE CHOOSES HIS LADY

Now that his armour was clean, his helmet made into a complete head-piece, a name found for his horse, and he confirmed in his new title, it struck him that there was only one more thing to do: to find a lady to be enamoured of. For a knight errant without a lady is like a tree without leaves or fruit and a body without a soul. He said to himself again and again: "If I for sins or by good luck were to meet with some giant hereabouts, as generally happens to knights errant, and if I were to overthrow him in the encounter, or cut him down the middle or, in short, conquer him and make him surrender, would it not be well to have someone to whom I could send him as a present, so that he could enter and kneel down before my sweet lady and say in tones of humble submission: 'Lady,

I am the giant Caraculiambro, lord of the island of Malindrania, whom the never-sufficiently-to-be-praised knight, Don Quixote de la Mancha, conquered in single combat and ordered to appear before your Grace, so that your Highness might dispose of me according to your will?' " Oh, how pleased our knight was when he had made up this speech, and even gladder when he found someone whom he could call his lady. It happened, it is believed, in this way: in a village near his there was a very good-looking farm girl, whom he had been taken with at one time, although she is supposed not to have known it or had proof of it. Her name was Aldonza Lorenzo, and she it was he thought fit to call the lady of his fancies; and, casting around for a name which should not be too far away from her own, yet suggest and imply a princess and great lady, he resolved to call her Dulcinea del Toboso—for she was a native of Toboso—a name which seemed to him as musical, strange and significant as those others that he had devised for himself and his possessions.

If Spanish customs are strange they seem nothing to those of the Spanish Gypsies, that astonishing people who spread to every part of Europe, claiming Christian charity because the infidel had turned them out of "Little Egypt", a country which never existed.

A GYPSY WEDDING

After much feasting, drinking, and yelling, in the Gypsy house, the bridal train sallied forth—a frantic spectacle. First of all marched a villainous jockey-looking fellow, holding in his hands, uplifted, a long pole, at the top of which fluttered in the morning air a snow-white cambric handkerchief, emblem of the bride's purity. Then came the betrothed pair, followed by their nearest friends; then a rabble rout of Gypsies, screaming and shouting, and discharging guns and pistols, till all around rang with the din, and the village dogs barked. On arriving at the church gate, the fellow who bore the pole stuck it into the ground with a loud huzza, and the train, forming two ranks, defiled into the church on either side of the pole and its strange ornaments. On the conclusion of the ceremony, they returned in the same manner in which they had come.

Throughout the day there was nothing going on but singing, drinking, feasting, and dancing; but the most singular part of the festival was reserved for the dark night. Nearly a ton weight of sweetmeats had been prepared, at an enormous expense, not for the gratification of the palate, but for a purpose purely

Gypsy. These sweetmeats of all kinds, and of all forms, but principally yémas, or yolks of eggs prepared with a crust of sugar (a delicious bonne-bouche), were strewn on the floor of a large room, at least to the depth of three inches. Into this room, at a given signal, tripped the bride and bridegroom *dancing románis*, followed amain by all the Gitános and Gitánas, *dancing románis*. To convey a slight idea of the scene is almost beyond the power of words. In a few minutes the sweetmeats were reduced to a powder, or rather to a mud, the dancers were soiled to the knees with sugar, fruits, and yolks of eggs. Still more terrific became the lunatic merriment. The men sprang high in the air, neighed, brayed, and crowed; whilst the Gitánas snapped their fingers in their own fashion, louder than castanets, distorting their forms into all kinds of obscene attitudes, and uttering words to repeat which were an abomination.

GEORGE BORROW *The Zincali*, 1841

The customs of courtship were not confined to conversations at the *rejas*. Gerald Brenan lived for many years in an Andalusian village near Granada.

SWEET BASIL

In my village it was the custom for girls to grow this plant in pots, and on Midsummer Day to present one of them to their young man or *novio*. They kept the pots on their balconies, and if a girl had no *novio* the youths who wished to court her would climb up at night, pick a piece of it and place it behind the ear. On the following day they would walk past her house wearing it in this manner so that she could see them. This was also done with *claveles* or carnations . . . and if no one stole a girl's pot-plants she would feel neglected.

South from Granada

How much of all this strange ritual survives today?

AND NOW

"In many books about Spain," I said, "you read that at night time in Andalusia the lover may be seen pressed against the iron window screens, whispering to his beloved. I have looked everywhere and not once have I seen this."

"Ah," they said, "it was so even to the outbreak of the Civil War, but, like so many other things in Spain, it went at that time. There is now no need for the lover to whisper through

55

the *rejas*; he can do so elsewhere, for the girls are no longer behind the screen."

"Yes, that is true," said someone, "and—there are many more illegitimate children!"

"I was talking to a priest the other day," said a third, "who was telling me how many more illegitimate children there are, and he said that during the Republic and the Civil War the Spanish girls achieved freedom much too quickly. He told me that recently a girl said to him that she was going to have a child and the father was a young soldier stationed in Seville, who was her *novio*. The priest asked her to bring the young man to see him, and the young man was glad to go. He told the priest he was much troubled in his mind because he had four other *novias* in various garrison towns of Spain, and each one had had a child, and his trouble was that he didn't know which one of his *novias* he ought to marry, because his love for them was equal. He begged the priest to advise him."

"And what did the priest do?"

"Well, what do they say in America? He passed the buck. He told the young man to go and confess his sins to his own village priest and ask *his* advice!"

"How interesting," said a fourth. "What would *you* advise him to do?"

"Well, it's a question," said a fifth, "whether first love or last love is the more enduring, and he must advise the young man to marry either the first *novia* or the last."

H. V. MORTON *A Stranger In Spain*

But there is still much that is superstitious, picturesque, and sometimes to a stranger embarrassing about the Spanish attitude to love, as these pieces, describing Spain in the last few years, show.

THE TUNA

The *tuna* came again last night to serenade one of the pretty girl students who live opposite me. There were about forty or fifty boys, dressed in black, with tight trousers, black stockings and shiny patent-leather shoes. Their black capes are tied at the shoulder with a bunch of multicoloured ribbons and they play tambourines, bandurias and guitars decorated with ribbons. They sing a mixture of songs, some classical, some modern, but all of them have something to do with love. The girls whom they are serenading come out on to their balcony and after a while, provided they know them of course, they are invited up for liqueurs and biscuits. It is all very gay and youthful.

56

FOR MONK OR MONARCH

A corner of the vast, gloomy Escorial, monastery-palace which Philip II built for himself fifty miles from Madrid, from which he "ruled the world with two inches of paper"

GIRLS AT A WINDOW

Courting may no longer be done by a young man in a cloak stand-ing in the street below the reja *of his* novia, *but a habit of looking down from behind the safety of an iron grill survives*

VIRGEN DE LOS DOLORES OF TOLEDO

This image is to be found in the Street of the Pins, *la calle de los Alfileres*. Legend says that a girl whose lover was sent away from the town bid him adieu in this street. Every time she passed through it she was so overcome by emotion that she felt like fainting. To prevent this from happening, she pricked herself with a pin. One day the Virgen de los Dolores appeared to her and said: "I too have suffered. Have patience. All will be well." A few days later the lover re-appeared and the pair were happily married. Since then the Virgen de los Dolores has become the patron of Toledan lovers who, when they pass before her image, drop a pin in a nearby groove in the wall accompanied by a petition. It is said that an average of between twenty to thirty pins a week are cast before the Toledan image during the winter months but that the quantity increases to between two and three hundred in the month of May.

NINA EPTON *Love and the Spanish*, 1961

PIROPO OR THE ART OF PUBLIC FLIRTATION

Andalusian witty flirtation is hard to rival and quite impossible to render in translation. It is the long-distance broadside of ships which are too far away from one another to close in and grapple. Knowing that they are not committing themselves, because Spanish courtship is so long and slow, both can indulge in intimate and extravagant fantasies in complete safety.

The *piropo*, the compliments which men shout in the street to passing girls, is part of the same thing. The men know that no girl but a whore will take them seriously; the girls know that actions will not follow words. But for a man it is pleasant to express appreciation openly and in as witty a manner as possible; while many a girl will return to her mirror and ask what is wrong if she goes out one morning and hears no *"Guapa"* or *"Qué mujer más hermosa!"*

JOHN HAYCRAFT *Babel in Spain*

And if you marry a Spaniard:

MY SHEETS

"My dear," she began, "you've no *idea* how cross the Mamás of Seville are with you! They're simply *furious!*"

"But why?"

Didn't I realise, she explained, the enormity of my misdemeanour—that I, a girl unknown, a foreigner, had walked off with one of the most eligible bachelors in the city? Moreover, I had seized this plum from under their very noses without even conforming in one single detail to the accepted pattern of Southern Spanish courtship.

I didn't know whether to be flattered or upset by this revelation, but before I could get a word in edgeways my friend was off again.

Where had been my chaperones? Why had I never worn the customary Spanish engagement bracelet? she enquired. What of the formal meetings and official arrangements between parents of both sides? And, she finished, rapping me on the knees with her fan for emphasis, where were my *sheets*?

"My—my sheets?" I faltered, staring. "We don't need any sheets while we're living in an hotel."

Only years later did I realise how sadly I had fallen out of line in this respect. No Spanish girl ever gets married without first preparing through the months—and maybe years—a vast trousseau of linen of every kind, all lovingly and laboriously made at home.

Eventually I came to judge how soon a servant would be likely to be leaving to get married by the state of her trousseau. While she was still collecting her sheets I knew I could bank on a certain amount of leeway, but once she had acquired her bedspread—the ultimate and most important item of her trousseau —then I knew the time had come to start looking for her successor.

BARBARA BORBOLLA Mantillas and Me, 1961

At War

The martial ardour and success of the Spaniards lasted for more than a thousand years; it was only at very great cost that the Romans subdued the Iberians, and down to the sixteenth century the Spaniards were great soldiers; but the struggle in the Netherlands against the Dutch finally wasted their energies, and when at Rocroy, in the middle of the seventeenth century, the Spanish infantry that had been counted the finest in Europe went down before the French, the military splendour of Spain finally vanished.

HAVELOCK ELLIS

Of all Spanish soldiers, Don John of Austria most successfully caught the public imagination of his time, and holds ours today. He was Philip II's bastard brother, son of a German merchant's daughter, and it was he who at the age of 26 led the Papal fleet at the great defeat of the Turks at Lepanto. The handsomest, most gallant man in Europe, as his fleet was about to engage the infidel he was seen on the gun platform of his flagship, in gold armour, dancing a galliard with two of his officers.

LEPANTO

White founts falling in the courts of the sun,
And the Soldan of Byzantium is smiling as they run;
There is laughter like the fountains in that face of all men
 feared,
It stirs the forest darkness, the darkness of his beard,
It curls the blood-red crescent, the crescent of his lips,
For the inmost sea of all the earth is shaken with his ships.
They have dared the white republics up the capes of Italy,
They have dashed the Adriatic round the Lion of the Sea,
And the Pope has cast his arms abroad for agony and loss,
And called the kings of Christendom for swords about the Cross,
The cold queen of England is looking in the glass;
The shadow of the Valois is yawning at the Mass;

From evening isles fantastical rings faint the Spanish gun,
And the Lord upon the Golden Horn is laughing in the sun.

Dim drums throbbing, in the hills half heard,
Where only on a nameless throne a crownless prince has
    stirred,
Where, risen from a doubtful seat and half-attainted stall,
The last knight of Europe takes weapons from the wall,
The last and lingering troubadour to whom the bird has sung,
That once went singing southward when all the world was
    young,
In that enormous silence, tiny and unafraid,
Comes up along a winding road the noise of the Crusade.
Strong gongs groaning as the guns boom far,
Don John of Austria is going to the war,
Stiff flags straining in the night-blasts cold
In the gloom black-purple, in the glint old-gold,
Torchlight crimson on the copper kettle-drums,
Then the tuckets, then the trumpets, then the cannon, and he
    comes.
Don John laughing in the brave beard curled,
Spurning of his stirrups like the thrones of all the world,
Holding his head up for a flag for all the free;
Love-light of Spain—hurrah!
Death-light of Africa!
Don John of Austria
Is riding to the sea.

               ★   ★   ★

King Philip's in his closet with the Fleece about his neck
(*Don John of Austria is armed upon the deck*).
The walls are hung with velvet that is black and soft as sin,
And little dwarfs creep out of it and little dwarfs creep in.
He holds a crystal phial that has colours like the moon,
He touches, and it tingles, and he trembles very soon,
And his face is as a fungus of a leprous white and grey
Like plants in the high houses that are shuttered from the day,
And death is in the phial, and the end of noble work,
But Don John of Austria has fired upon the Turk.
Don John's hunting, and his hounds have brayed—
Booms away past Italy the rumour of his raid.
Gung upon gun, Ha! ha!
Gun upon gun, hurrah!
Don John of Austria
Has loosed his cannonade.

               ★   ★   ★

Don John pounding from the slaughter-painted poop,

Purpling all the ocean like a bloody pirate's sloop,
Scarlet running over on the silvers and the golds,
Breaking of the hatches up and bursting of the holds,
Thronging of the thousands up that labour under sea
White for bliss and blind for sun and stunned for liberty.
Vivat Hispania!
Domino Gloria!
Don John of Austria
Has set his people free!

Cervantes on his galley sets the sword back in the sheath
(*Don John of Austria rides homeward with a wreath*)
And he sees across a weary land a straggling road in Spain,
Up which a lean and foolish knight forever rides in vain,
And he smiles, but not as Sultans smile, and settles back the
　　　blade . . .
(*But Don John of Austria rides home from the Crusade*).

G. K. CHESTERTON

It was at this battle that Cervantes lost the use of his
left hand, but luckily not that of his right.

Don John came to a less happy end. Sent to govern
the Spanish Netherlands, he died of typhoid six years
later. So that he could be buried at the Escorial, and
to avoid the cost of moving a royal body in state across
France, he was cut into three pieces, sewn into three
leather saddle-bags, and smuggled home.

Lepanto was won by oared galleys, the traditional
warships of the Mediterranean. In the vital years at
the end of the sixteenth century Spain's ocean-going
ships were no match for the English fleet—or for
Drake's unauthorized tactics.

OF THE NOTABLE SERVICE PERFORMED BY SIR FRANCIS DRAKE UPON THE SPANISH FLEET PREPARED IN THE ROAD OF CADIZ

Her Majestie being informed of a mightie preparation by Sea
begunne in Spaine for the invasion of England, by good advise
of her grave and prudent Counsell thought it expedient to
prevent the same. Whereupon she caused a Fleete of some 30.
sailes to be rigged and furnished with all things necessary. Over
the fleete she appointed Generall sir Francis Drake. . . .

The 16. of the said moneth we mette in the latitude of 40.

degrees with two ships of Middleborough, which came from Cadiz; by which we understood that there was great store of warlike provision at Cadiz & thereabout ready to come for Lisbon. Upon this information our Generall with al speed possible, bending himselfe thither to cut off their said forces and provisions, upon the 19. of April entered with his Fleet into the harbour of Cadiz: where at our first entring we were assailed over against the Towne by sixe Gallies, which notwithstanding in short time retired under their fortresse.

There were in the Road 60. ships and divers other small vessels under the fortresse: there fled about 20. French ships to Port Real, and some small Spanish vessels that might passe the sholdes. At our first comming in we sunk with our shot a ship of Raguza of 1000. tunnes, furnished with 40. pieces of brasse and very richly laden. There came two Gallies more from S. Mary port, and two from Porto Reale, which shot freely at us, but altogether in vaine: for they went away with the bowes well beaten for their paines.

Before night we had taken 30. of the said ships, & became Masters of the Road, in despight of the Gallies, which were glad to retire them under the Fort: in the number of which ships there was one new ship of an extraordinary hugenesse in burthen above 1200. tunnes, belonging to the Marquesse of Santa Cruz being at that instant high Admiral of Spaine. Five of them were great ships of Biskay, whereof 4. we fired, as they were taking in the Kings provision of victuals for the furnishing of his Fleet at Lisbon: the fift being a ship of about 1000. tunnes in burthen, laden with Iron-spikes, nailes, yron hoopes, horse-shooes, and other like necessaries bound for the West Indies we fired in like maner. Also we took a ship of 250. tunnes laden with wines for the Kings provision, which wee caried out to Sea with us, and there discharged the said wines for our owne store, and afterwards set her on fire. Moreover we tooke 3. Flyboats of 300. tunnes a piece laden with biscuit, whereof one was halfe unladen by us in Harborow, and there fired, and the other two we tooke in our company to Sea. Likewise there were fired by us ten other ships which were laden with wine, raisins, figs, oiles, wheat, and such like. To conclude, the whole number of ships and barkes (as we suppose) then burnt, suncke, and brought away with us amounted to 30. at the least, being (in our judgement) about 10000. tunnes of shipping. . . .

We found little ease during our aboad there, by reason of their continual shooting from the Gallies, the fortresses, and from the shoare: where continually at places convenient they planted new ordinance to offend us with: besides the inconvenience which wee suffered from their ships, which, when they could defend no longer, they set on fire to come among us. Whereupon when the flood came wee were not a little troubled to defend us from their terrible fire, which neverthelesse was a pleasant sight for us to beholde, because we were thereby eased of a great labour, which lay upon us day and night, in discharging the victuals, and other provisions of the enemie. Thus by the assistance of the Almightie, and the invincible courage and industrie of our Generall, this strange and happy enterprize was achieved in one day and two nights, to the great astonishment of the King of Spaine, which bread such a corrasive in the heart of the Marques of Santa Cruz high Admiral of Spaine, that he never enjoyed good day after, but within fewe moneths (as may justly be supposed) died of extreame griefe and sorrow.

Thus having performed this notable service, we came out of the Road of Cadiz on the Friday morning the 21. of the said moneth of April, with very small losse not worth mentioning.

RICHARD HAKLUYT *Voyages and Documents*, 1589

Any account of the Spanish at war must include the Conquistadors, those few hundred Spanish who conquered a continent. W. H. Prescott, the American historian who wrote these vivid descriptions, never went to Central America, was blind in one eye from Harvard days when he was hit by a bread pellet at a rag, and had such poor sight in the other that he could only work on *The Conquest of Mexico* for an hour a day, in two half-hour periods. He wrote fifteen other voluminous works of history.

Reaching Mexico in 1519, Herman Cortés sailed up the coast, engaging the Indians at various places. By the time he had established a base at Vera Cruz and before he had even begun his march to the Aztec capital his troops were restless.

A DARING RESOLUTION

The affair of the conspiracy seems to have made a deep impression on his mind. It showed him that there were timid spirits in the camp on whom he could not rely, and who, he feared, might spread the seeds of disaffection among their companions. Even the more resolute, on any occasion of disgust or disappointment hereafter, might falter in purpose, and, getting possession of the vessels, abandon the enterprise. . . . He came to the daring resolution to destroy the fleet, without the knowledge of his army.

When arrived at Cempoalla, he communicated his design to a few of his devoted adherents, who entered warmly into his views. Through them he readily persuaded the pilots, by means of those golden arguments which weigh more than any other with ordinary minds, to make such a report of the condition of the fleet as suited his purpose. The ships, they said, were grievously racked by the heavy gales they had encountered, and, what was worse, the worms had eaten into their sides and bottoms until most of them were not sea-worthy, and some indeed, could scarcely now be kept afloat.

Cortés received the communication with surprise; "for he could well dissemble," observes Las Casas, with his usual friendly comment, "when it suited his interest." "If it be so," he exclaimed, "we must make the best of it! Heaven's will be done!" He then ordered five of the worst-conditioned to be dismantled, their cordage, sails, iron, and whatever was moveable, to be brought on shore, and the ships to be sunk. A survey was made of the others, and, on a similar report, four more were condemned in the same manner. Only one small vessel remained!

When the intelligence reached the troops in Cempoalla, it caused the deepest consternation. They saw themselves cut off by a single blow from friends, family, country! The stoutest hearts quailed before the prospect of being thus abandoned on a hostile shore, a handful of men arrayed against a formidable empire. When the news arrived of the destruction of the five vessels first condemned, they had acquiesced in it, as a necessary measure, knowing the mischievous activity of the insects in these tropical seas. But, when this was followed by the loss of the remaining four, suspicions of the truth flashed on their minds. They felt they were betrayed. Murmurs, at first deep, swelled louder and louder, menacing open mutiny. "Their general," they said, "had led them like cattle to be butchered in the shambles!" The affair wore a most alarming aspect. In no situation was Cortés ever exposed to greater danger from his soldiers.

His presence of mind did not desert him at this crisis. He called his men together, and employing the tones of persuasion rather than authority, assured them that a survey of the ships showed they were not fit for service. If he had ordered them to be destroyed, they should consider, also, that his was the greatest sacrifice, for they were his property,—all, indeed, he possessed in the world. . . . "As for me," he concluded, "I have chosen my part. I will remain here, while there is one to bear me company. If there be any so craven, as to shrink from sharing the dangers of our glorious enterprise, let them go home, in God's name. There is still one vessel left. Let them take that and return to Cuba. They can tell there how they deserted their commander and their comrades, and patiently wait till we return loaded with the spoils of the Aztecs."

The politic orator had touched the right chord in the bosoms of the soldiers. As he spoke, their resentment gradually died away. The faded visions of future riches and glory, rekindled by his eloquence, again floated before their imaginations. The first shock over, they felt ashamed of their temporary distrust. The enthusiasm for their leader revived, for they felt that under his banner only they could hope for victory; and they testified the revulsion of their feelings by making the air ring with their shouts, "To Mexico! to Mexico!"

After many battles and adventures his tiny force reached Tlacopan, or Mexico city as it became, and were welcomed by the emperor Montezuma who believed them to be gods. But the temptation of the Aztec treasure was too great. Intrigue, plot and revolt followed till at last the city had to be evacuated.

NOCHE TRISTE

Much of the treasure belonging to the crown and to individuals was necessarily abandoned, from the want of adequate means of conveyance. The metal lay scattered in shining heaps along the floor, exciting the cupidity of the soldiers. "Take what you will of it," said Cortés to his men. "Better you should have it than these Mexican hounds. But be careful not to overload yourselves. He travels safest in the dark night who travels lightest." His own more wary followers took heed to this counsel, helping themselves to a few articles of least bulk, though, it might be, of greatest value. But the troops of Narvaez, pining for riches, of which they had heard so much, and hitherto seen so little, showed no such discretion. To them it seemed as if the very mines of Mexico were turned up before them, and, rushing on the treacherous spoil, they greedily loaded themselves with as much of it, not merely as they could accommodate about their persons, but as they could stow away in wallets, boxes, or any other mode of conveyance at their disposal. . . .

The night was cloudy, and a drizzling rain, which fell without intermission, added to the obscurity. The great square before the palace was deserted, as, indeed, it had been since the fall of Montezuma. Steadily, and as noiselessly as possible, the Spaniards held their way along the great street of Tlacopan, which so lately had resounded to the tumult of battle. . . . The city slept undisturbed even by the prolonged echoes of the tramp of horses, and the hoarse rumbling of the artillery and baggage trains. At length a lighter space beyond the dusky line of buildings showed the van of the army that it was emerging on the open causeway. They might well have congratulated themselves on having thus escaped the dangers of an assault in the city itself, and that a brief time would place them in comparative safety on the opposite shore. But the Mexicans were not all asleep.

As the Spaniards drew near the spot where the street opened on the causeway, and were preparing to lay the portable bridge across the uncovered breach which now met their eyes, several Indian sentinels, who had been stationed at this, as at the other approaches to the city, took alarm, and fled, rousing their countrymen by their cries. The priests, keeping their night watch on the summit of the *teocallis*, instantly caught the tidings and sounded their shells, while the huge drum in the desolate temple of the war-god sent forth those solemn tones, which, heard only in seasons of calamity, vibrated through every corner of the capital. The Spaniards saw that no time was to be lost. The bridge was brought forward and fitted with all possible expedition. Sandoval was the first to try its strength, and, riding across, was followed by his little body of chivalry, his infantry, and Tlascalan allies, who formed the first division of the army. Then came Cortés and his squadrons, with the baggage, ammunition waggons, and a part of the artillery. But before they had time to defile across the narrow passage, a gathering sound was heard, like that of a mighty forest agitated by the winds. It grew louder and louder, while on the dark waters of the lake was heard a splashing noise, as of many oars. Then came a few stones and arrows striking at random among the hurrying troops. They fell every moment faster and more furious, till they thickened into a terrible tempest, while the very heavens were rent with the yells and war-cries of myriads of combatants, who seemed all at once to be swarming over land and lake.

The Spaniards pushed steadily on through this arrowy sleet, though the barbarians, dashing their canoes against the side of the causeway, clambered up and broke in upon their ranks. But the Christians, anxious only to make their escape, declined combat except for self-preservation. The cavaliers, spurring forward their steeds, shook off their assailants, and rode over their prostrate bodies, while the men on foot with their good swords or the butts of their pieces drove them headlong again down the sides of the dike.

But the advance of several thousand men, marching, probably, on a front of not more than fifteen or twenty abreast, necessarily required much time, and the leading files had already reached the second breach in the causeway before those in the rear had entirely traversed the first. Hence they halted; as they had no means of effecting a passage, smarting all the while under unintermitting volleys from the enemy, who were clustered thick on the waters around this second opening. Sorely distressed, the vanguard sent repeated messages to the rear to demand the portable bridge. At length the last of the army had crossed, and Magarino and his sturdy followers endeavoured to raise the ponderous framework. But it stuck fast in the sides of the dike. In vain they strained every nerve. The weight of so many men and horses, and above all of the heavy artillery, had wedged the timbers so firmly in the stones and earth, that it was beyond their power to dislodge them. Still they laboured amidst a torrent of missiles, until, many of them slain, and all wounded, they were obliged to abandon the attempt.

The tidings soon spread from man to man, and no sooner was their dreadful import comprehended, than a cry of despair arose, which for a moment drowned all the noise of conflict. All means of retreat were cut off. Scarcely hope was left. The only hope was in such desperate exertions as each could make for himself. Order and subordination were at an end. Intense danger produced intense selfishness. Each thought only of his own life. Pressing forward, he trampled down the weak and the wounded, heedless whether it were friend or foe. The leading files, urged on by the rear, were crowded on the brink of the gulf. Sandoval, Ordaz, and the other cavaliers dashed into the water. Some succeeded in swimming their horses across; others failed, and some, who reached the opposite bank, being overturned in the ascent, rolled headlong with their steeds into the lake. The infantry followed pellmell, heaped promiscuously on one another, frequently pierced by the shafts, or struck down by the war-clubs of the Aztecs; while many an unfortunate victim was dragged half-stunned on board their canoes, to be reserved for a protracted, but more dreadful death.

The carnage raged fearfully along the length of the causeway. Its shadowy bulk presented a mark of sufficient distinctness for the enemy's missiles, which often prostrated their own countrymen in the blind fury of the tempest. Those nearest the dike, running their canoes alongside, with a force that shattered them to pieces, leaped on the land and grappled with the Christians, until both came rolling down the side of the causeway together. But the Aztec fell among his friends, while his antagonist was borne away in triumph to the sacrifice. The struggle was long and deadly. The Mexicans were recognised by their white cotton tunics, which showed faint through the darkness. Above the combatants rose a wild and discordant clamour, in which horrid shouts of vengeance were mingled with groans of agony, with invocations of the saints and the blessed Virgin, and with the screams of women; for there were several women, both native and Spaniards, who had accompanied the Christian camp. Among these, one named María de Estrada is particularly noticed for the courage she displayed, battling with the broadsword and target like the staunchest of the warriors.

The opening in the causeway, meanwhile, was filled up with the wreck of matter which had been forced into it, ammunition waggons, heavy guns, bales of rich stuffs scattered over the waters, chests of solid gold ingots, and bodies of men and horses, till over this dismal ruin a passage was gradually formed, by which those in the rear were enabled to clamber to the other side. Cortés, it is said, found a place that was fordable, where halting with the water up to his saddle-girths, he endeavoured to check the confusion, and lead his followers by a safer path to the opposite bank. But his voice was lost in the wild uproar, and finally, hurrying on with the tide, he pressed forwards with a few trusty cavaliers, who remained near his person, to the van; but not before he had seen his favourite page, Juan de Salazar, struck down, a corpse, by his side. Here he found Sandoval and his companions, halting before the third and last breach, endeavouring to cheer on their followers to surmount it. But their resolution faltered. It was wide and deep; though the passage was not so closely beset by the enemy as the preceding ones. The cavaliers again set the example by plunging into the water. Horse and foot followed as they could, some swimming, others with dying grasp clinging to the manes and tails of the struggling animals. Those fared best, as the general had predicted, who travelled lightest; and many were the unfortunate wretches, who, weighed down by the fatal gold which they loved so well, were buried with it in the salt floods of the lake. Cortés, with his gallant comrades, Olid, Morla, Sandoval, and some few others, still kept in the advance, leading his broken remnant off the fatal causeway. The din of battle lessened in the distance; when the rumour reached them, that the rear-guard would be wholly overwhelmed without speedy relief. It seemed almost an act of desperation; but the generous hearts of the Spanish cavaliers did not stop to calculate the danger when the cry for succour reached them. Turning their horses' bridles, they galloped back to the theatre of action, worked their way through the press, swam the canal, and placed themselves in the thick of the *mêlée* on the opposite bank.

The first grey of the morning was now coming over the waters. It showed the hideous confusion of the scene which had been

68

shrouded in the obscurity of night. The dark masses of combatants, stretching along the dike, were seen struggling for
mastery, until the very causeway on which they stood appeared
to tremble, and reel to and fro, as if shaken by an earthquake;
while the bosom of the lake, as far as the eye could reach, was
darkened by canoes crowded with warriors, whose spears and
bludgeons, armed with blades of "volcanic glass," gleamed in
the morning light.

W. H. PRESCOTT *The Conquest of Mexico*, 1843

Horses have always been a Spanish status-symbol. A
Spanish gentleman is a *caballero*—or horseman. In the
conquests of Southern America the horse was vital.
The Indians had never seen such a creature before, and
when they at last killed one they had its head sent
round the country to prove that it was not immortal.

FOR, AFTER GOD, WE OWED THE VICTORY TO THE HORSES

At the time of the conquest, there were two styles of riding
used in Spain. The first was known as "á la brida," and was in
fact the ancient style of riding practised by the knights.

In the Bur saddle as it was called, the horseman sat erect,
riding with long stirrup leathers. The saddle itself had a low
cantle, a small pommel and wings that served to press the
rider's knees against, after the fashion of an Australian stock-
rider's saddle, or that of the old knights. It was well padded in
the seat.

The other school, known as "á la gineta" was entirely
different. When the Moors were expelled from Spain, they left
their saddles and their style of riding. In the long centuries of
their domination, and the fierce warfare that preceded their
expulsion, Christians no doubt mastered both ways of riding.

So much importance did they attach to their double mastery,
that it became the highest praise to call a gallant cavalier, "a
man who could ride well in both saddles."

Sometimes the fact was even cut upon men's tombstones,
and served well, or better, than an ordinary epitaph. . . .

For all that the position of the Moors, with the short stirrups
and the legs bent backwards so as to give the appearance of
almost kneeling on the horse's back, was the style most affected
by the Conquistadores of America. This style they persevered in
both in the conquests of Peru and Mexico, and only by degrees
were forced to alter, or at least to moderate it, when horses

became numerous and wild. Then they found that with the short stirrup leathers, they were unable either to get upon a horse difficult to mount, or to remain upon the back of a wild bucking colt. . . .

With the high Moorish saddle, the rider used the powerful Moorish bit, a single rein, and always rode with rather a high hand.

The reason was that the horses were all bitted on the neck and not by pulling at the corners of the mouth, after the fashion of the northern Europeans. . . . A horse turned far more rapidly, and suffered less under this system, and turning quickly was the first essential for a warhorse in those days.

Those who have seen a Mexican, a Western cowboy, or a Gaucho turn his horse, chasing wild cattle, have seen the way in which the Conquistadores rode, for Mexicans and cowboys all ride with the high hand and palate bit, on almost the same saddle used by the conquerors.

R. B. CUNNINGHAM GRAHAM *The Horses of the Conquest*, 1930

Considering Spain's geographical isolation it is surprising how often Europe has fought its wars here. In the long struggle with the infidel, Spanish knights were excused the crusades because they had their own crusade at home. In 1366 the roving companies of British and French knights and archers came to Spain to restore Don Pedro of Castile to his throne, usurped by his brother Henry the bastard. Leading them was our own Black Prince.

THE GREAT BATTLE OF NAJARA

The Saturday in the morning between Nazres and Navaret was the battle right fell and cruel, and many a man brought to great mischief. There was done many a noble deed of arms by the prince and by the duke of Lancaster his brother . . . and the good knights and squires of France that were there acquitted themselves nobly: for in truth, if the Spaniards had done their part as well as the Frenchmen did, the Englishmen and Gascons should have had much more to do and have suffered more pain than they did. The fault was not in king Henry that they did no better, for he had well admonished and desired them to have done their devoir valiantly, and so they had promised him to have done. The king bare himself right valiantly, and did marvels in arms, and with good courage comforted his people, as, when they were flying and opening, he came in among them and said: "Lords, I am your king: ye have made me king of Castile, and have sworn and promised that to die ye will not fail me. For God's sake keep your promise that ye have sworn, and acquit you against me, and I shall acquit me against you; for I shall not fly one foot as long as I may see you do your devoir." By these words and such other full of comfort king Henry brought his men together again three times the same day, and with his own hands he fought valiantly, so that he ought greatly to be honoured and renowned.

This was a marvellous dangerous battle, and many a man slain and sore hurt. The commons of Spain according to the usage of their country with their slings they did cast stones with great violence and did much hurt, the which at the beginning troubled greatly the Englishmen: but when their cast was past and that they felt the sharp arrows light among them, they could no longer keep their array. With king Henry in his battle were many noble men of arms, as well of Spain as of Lisbon, of Aragon and of Portugal, who acquitted them right nobly and gave it not up so lightly, for valiantly they fought with spears, javelins, archegayes and swords; and on the wing of king Henry's battle there were certain well mounted, who always kept the battle in good order, for if the battle opened or brake array in any side, then they were ever ready to help to bring them into good order. So these Englishmen and Gascons, or they had the advantage, they bought it dearly, and won it by noble chivalry and great prowess of arms; and for to say truth, the prince himself was the chief flower of chivalry of all the world, and had with him as then right noble and valiant knights and squires. . . . There was none that fained to fight valiantly, and also they had good cause why; for there were of Spaniards and of Castile more than a hundred thousand men in harness, so that by reason of their great number it was long or they could be overcome. King don Peter was greatly chafed, and much desired to meet with the bastard his brother, and said: "Where is that whoreson that calleth himself king of Castile?" And the same king Henry fought right valiantly whereas he was, and held his people together right marvellously, and said: "Ah! ye good people, ye have crowned me king, therefore help and aid me to keep the heritage that you have given me." So that by these words and such other as he spake that day he caused many to be right hardy and valiant, whereby they abode on the field, so that because of their honour they would not fly from the place.

When . . . the Spaniards could not sustain nor defend them any longer, but began to fly away in great fear without any good array . . . so that for any words that king Henry could say they would not return, then he called for his horse and mounted thereon and put himself among them that fled. . . . Then the Englishmen and Gascons leapt a-horseback and began to chase the Spaniards, who fled away sore discomfited to the great river. And at the entry of the bridge of Nazres there was a hideous shedding of blood, and many a man slain and drowned; for divers leapt into the water, the which was deep and hideous; they thought they had as lief to be drowned as slain. And in this chase among other there were two valiant knights of Spain bearing on them the habit of religion, the one called the great prior of Saint James and the other the great master of Calatrava; they and their company to save themselves entered into Nazres . . . and the Englishmen entered into the city after their enemies, who were entered into a strong house of stone. Howbeit, incontinent it was won by force, and the knights taken and many of their men slain and all the city overrun and pilled, the which was greatly to England's profit. Also they won king Henry's lodging, wherein they found great riches of vessel and jewels of gold and silver; for the king was come thither with great nobleness, so that when they were discomfited, they had no leisure for to return thither again to save that they had left there. So this was a hideous and terrible discomfiture, and specially on the river side there was many a man slain; and it was said, as I heard after reported of some of them that were there present, that one might have seen the water that ran by Nazres to be of the colour of red with the blood of men and horses that were slain. This battle was between Nazres and Navaret in Spain the year of the incarnation of our Lord Jesu Christ a thousand three hundred threescore and six, the third day of April, the which was on a Saturday.

The Chronicles of Froissart, trans. Lord Berners

In Spain for the Peninsular War, the Duke of Wellington took a severe view of his Spanish allies.

SPANISH CAVALRY

The Spanish cavalry are, I believe, nearly without discipline. They are in general well clothed, armed, and accoutred, and remarkably well mounted . . . but I have never heard anybody pretend that in any one instance they had behaved as soldiers should in the presence of an enemy. They make no scruple of running off, and after an action are to be found in every shady bottom within fifty miles of the field of battle.

Despatch, 1809

1936

The most famous picture to come out of the Civil War.
Robert Capa's camera catches a soldier at the very moment of
death, as he is killed by a machine-gun bullet through the head

JOIN US FOR A GOSSIP

*A cool back street in the small town of Haro in
Old Castile. Just the place to exchange the news*

As the Moorish wars were a Christian crusade, so the Spanish Civil War became to the 'thirties a crusade against Fascism, a test case in which all could prove their beliefs in action. Unfashionable as it is to say so, I was on Franco's side. I can remember my father telling us how the Reds had burnt the churches, in the resigned tone he used about symptoms of world deterioration which were too distant to grow too angry about.

THE CIVIL WAR

On that arid square, that fragment nipped off from hot
Africa, soldered so crudely to inventive Europe;
      On that tableland scored by rivers,
Our thoughts have bodies; the menacing shapes of our fever

Are precise and alive. For the fears which made us respond
To the medicine ad. and the brochure of winter cruises
      Have become invading battalions;
And our faces, the institute-face, the chain-store, the ruin

Are projecting their greed as the firing squad and the bomb.
Madrid is the heart. Our moments of tenderness blossom
      As the ambulance and the sandbag;
Our hours of friendship into a people's army.

W. H. AUDEN Spain

No one has caught better the excitement of the early days in Madrid than André Malraux in his novel *L'Espoir*. Malraux himself fought for the Government as a pilot.

THE REVOLUTION BREAKS

All Madrid was astir in the warm summer night, loud with the rumble of lorries stacked with rifles. For some days the Workers' Organizations had been announcing that a Fascist rising might take place at any moment, that the soldiers in the barracks had been "got at", and munitions were pouring in. At 1 a.m. the Government decided to arm the people, and from 3 a.m. the production of a union-card entitled every member to be issued with a rifle. It was high time, for the reports telephoned in from the provinces, which had sounded hopeful between midnight and 2 a.m., were beginning to strike a different note.

The Central Exchange at the Northern Railway Terminus
rang up the various stations along the line. Ramos, the Secretary
of the Railway Workers' Union, and Manuel were in charge.
With the exception of Navarre—the line from which had been
cut—the replies had been uniform. Either the Government had
the situation well in hand, or a Workers' Committee had taken
charge of the city, pending instructions from the central
authority. But now a change was coming over the dialogues.

"Is that Huesca?"

"Who's speaking?"

"The Workers' Committee, Madrid."

"Not for long, you swine! *Arriba España!*"

Fixed to the wall by drawing-pins, the special late edition
of the *Claridad* flaunted a caption six columns wide: *Comrades
To Arms!*

"Hallo, Avila? How's things at your end? Madrid North
speaking."

"The hell it is, you bastards! *Viva El Cristo Rey!*"

"See you soon. *Salud!*"

An urgent message was put through to Ramos.

The Northern lines linked up with Saragossa, Burgos, and
Valladolid.

"Is that Saragossa? Put me through to the Workers' Committee at the station."

"We've shot them. Your turn next. *Arriba España!*"

"Hullo, Tablada! Madrid North here, Union Delegate."

"Call the jail, you son of a gun. That's where your friends
are. And we'll be coming for you in a day or two; we want to
have a word with you."

"*Bueno!* Let's meet on the Alcala, second dive on the left.
Got it?"

All the telephone operators were staring at Manuel, whose
devil-may-care manner, curly hair, and grin gave him the air
of a jovial gangster.

"Hallo, is that Burgos?"

"Commandante, Burgos, speaking."

Ramos hung up.

A telephone-bell rang.

"Hallo, Madrid! Who's there?"

"Railway Workers' Union."

"Miranda speaking. We hold the station and the town. *Arriba
España!*"

"But *we* hold Madrid. *Salud!*"

So there was no counting on help from the North, except by
way of Valladolid. Remained the Asturias.

"Is that Oviedo? Yes ? Who's speaking?" Ramos was getting
wary.

"Workers' Delegate. Railway Station."

"Ramos here, the Union Secretary. How are things your end?"

"Aranda's loyal to the Government. It's touch and go at Valladolid. We're entraining three thousand armed miners to reinforce our lot."

"When?" A clash of rifle-butts drowned the answer. Ramos repeated the question.

"At once."

"*Salud!*"

Ramos turned to Manuel. "Keep in touch with that train, by telephone." Then called Valladolid.

"Is that Valladolid?"

"Who's speaking?"

"Station Delegate."

"How's it going?"

"Our fellows hold the barracks. We're expecting a reinforcement from Oviedo. Do your best to get them here as soon as possible. But don't you worry; here it'll all go well. What about you?"

They were singing outside the station; Ramos could not hear himself speak.

"What?" Valladolid repeated.

"Going well! Going well!"

"Have the troops revolted?"

"Not yet."

Valladolid hung up.

George Orwell's experiences in the P.O.U.M. (a dissident Communist party opposed to Stalinism) on the Aragon front were not typical, but he more than anyone else has given me the feeling of the enthusiasm of the time, and of what it was like to be there.

BRAVER THAN WE ARE

But I would sooner be a foreigner in Spain than in most countries. How easy it is to make friends in Spain! Within a day or two there was a score of militiamen who called me by my Christian name, showed me the ropes and overwhelmed me with hospitality. I am not writing a book of propaganda and I do not want to idealize the P.O.U.M. militia. The whole militia-system had serious faults, and the men themselves were a mixed lot, for by this time voluntary recruitment was falling off and many of the best men were already at the front or dead.

75

There was always among us a certain percentage who were completely useless. Boys of fifteen were being brought up for enlistment by their parents, quite openly for the sake of the ten pesetas a day which was the militiaman's wage; also for the sake of the bread which the militia received in plenty and could smuggle home to their parents. But I defy anyone to be thrown among the Spanish working class—I ought perhaps to say Catalan working class, for apart from a few Aragonese and Andalusians I mixed only with Catalans—and not be struck by their essential decency; above all, their straightforwardness and generosity. A Spaniard's generosity, in the ordinary sense of the word, is at times almost embarrassing. If you ask him for a cigarette he will force the whole packet upon you. And beyond this there is generosity in a deeper sense, a real largeness of spirit, which I have met with again and again in the most unpromising circumstances. Some journalists and other foreigners who travelled in Spain during the war have declared that in secret the Spaniards were bitterly jealous of foreign aid. All I can say is that I never observed anything of the kind. I remember that a few days before I left the barracks a group of men returned on leave from the front. They were talking excitedly about their experiences and were full of enthusiasm for some French troops who had been next to them at Huesca. The French were very brave, they said; adding enthusiastically: "Mas valientes que nosotros"—"Braver than we are!" Of course I demurred, whereupon they explained that the French knew more of the art of war—were more expert with bombs, machine-guns, and so forth. Yet the remark was significant. An Englishman would cut his hand off sooner than say a thing like that.

Every foreigner who served in the militia spent his first few weeks in learning to love the Spaniards and in being exasperated by certain of their characteristics. In the front line my own exasperation sometimes reached the pitch of fury. The Spaniards are good at many things, but not at making war. All foreigners alike are appalled by their maddening unpunctuality. The one Spanish word that no foreigner can avoid learning is *mañana*— "tomorrow" (literally, "the morning"). Whenever it is conceivably possible, the business of today is put off until *mañana*. This is so notorious that even the Spaniards themselves make jokes about it. In Spain nothing, from a meal to a battle, ever happens at the appointed time. As a general rule things happen too late, but just occasionally—just so that you shan't even be able to depend on their happening late—they happen too early. A train which is due to leave at eight will normally leave at any time between nine and ten, but perhaps once a week, thanks to some private whim of the engine-driver, it leaves at half-past seven. Such things can be a little trying. In theory I rather admire the Spaniards for not sharing our Northern time-neurosis; but unfortunately I share it myself.

THE ARAGON FRONT

Whenever the lines were within hailing distance of one another there was always a good deal of shouting from trench to trench. From ourselves: "Fascistas—maricones!" From the Fascists: "Viva España! Viva Franco!"—or, when they knew that there were English opposite them: "Go home, you English! We don't want foreigners here!" On the Government side, in the party militias, the shouting of propaganda to undermine the enemy morale had been developed into a regular technique. In every suitable position men, usually machine-gunners, were told off for shouting-duty and provided with megaphones. Generally they shouted a set-piece, full of revolutionary senti-ments which explained to the Fascist soldiers that they were merely hirelings of international capitalism, that they were fighting against their own class, etc., etc., and urged them to come over to our side. This was repeated over and over by relays of men; sometimes it continued almost the whole night. There is very little doubt that it had its effect. . . . But at the beginning it dismayed all of us; it made us feel that the Spaniards were not taking this war of theirs sufficiently seriously. The man who did the shouting at the P.S.U.C. post down on our right was an artist at the job. Sometimes, instead of shouting revolutionary slogans he simply told the Fascists how much better we were fed than they were. His account of the Government rations was apt to be a little imaginative. "Buttered toast!"—you could hear his voice echoing across the lonely valley—"We're just sitting down to buttered toast over here! Lovely slices of buttered toast!"

Homage to Catalonia, 1938

In Barcelona Orwell took part in the most astonishing episode of an astonishing war, when three separate groups of Government supporters fought each other in the streets.

THE BARRICADES

The Barcelona streets are paved with square cobbles, easily built up into a wall, and under the cobbles is a kind of shingle that is good for filling sand-bags. The building of those barri-cades was a strange and wonderful sight; I would have given something to be able to photograph it. With the kind of

77

passionate energy that Spaniards display when they have definitely decided to begin upon any job of work, long lines of men, women, and quite small children were tearing up the cobblestones, hauling them along in a hand-cart that had been found somewhere, and staggering to and fro under heavy sacks of sand. In the doorway of the Comite Local a German-Jewish girl, in a pair of militiaman's trousers whose knee-buttons just reached her ankles, was watching with a smile. In a couple of hours the barricades were head-high, with riflemen posted at the loopholes, and behind one barricade a fire was burning and men were frying eggs. . . .

I used to sit on the roof marvelling at the folly of it all. From the little windows in the observatory you could see for miles around—vista after vista of tall slender buildings, glass domes and fantastic curly roofs with brilliant green and copper tiles; over to eastward the glittering pale blue sea—the first glimpse of the sea that I had had since coming to Spain. And the whole huge town of a million people was locked in a sort of violent inertia, a nightmare of noise without movement. The sunlit streets were quite empty. Nothing was happening except the streaming of bullets from barricades and sand-bagged windows. Not a vehicle was stirring in the streets; here and there along the Ramblas the trams stood motionless where their drivers had jumped out of them when the fighting started. And all the while the devilish noise, echoing from thousands of stone buildings, went on and on and on, like a tropical rainstorm. Crack-crack, rattle-rattle, roar—sometimes it died away to a few shots, sometimes it quickened to a deafening fusillade, but it never stopped while daylight lasted, and punctually next dawn is started again.

What the devil was happening, who was fighting whom and who was winning, was at first very difficult to discover. . . .

Homage to Catalonia

In Toledo the Alcazar, a military college, was defended by a few hundred civilians and cadets who were not on holiday against all Government efforts to destroy it, till it was reduced to rubble. Franco said later that relieving it instead of marching on Madrid cost him a year of war. The ruins of the Alcazar were left more or less as they were after the battle, and when I was last there the famous telephone conversation was framed in several languages on the walls of Colonel Moscardó's office, and the portrait of his son had been given a faint halo.

Now occurred an incident which was typical of what was happening all over Spain. But, because it was typical, it may help us to understand how this struggle came later to be conducted with terrible ruthlessness. At 10 a.m. Colonel Moscardó was called to his office, as the chief of the local Workers' Militia wished to speak to him over the telephone.

I know the room in which he received this communication. Being on the south face of the Alcazar it had not suffered greatly from shell-fire and, when I first saw it, was much as it must have been on that July morning.

The room was low, hung with torn terracotta wall-paper. It was ugly but full of character; part of a reconstruction undertaken after a fire in the 'eighties. There was a vast knee-hole desk, a revolving chair; the uninspiring equipment of a Government office. Hiding one corner was a built-in settee, the back of which, carried to some height, formed a screen. It was L-shaped, and above the imitation leather upholstery were chestnut-wood panels, each of which enclosed an enlarged photograph of some past colonel-commandant of the Academy. In a building so palatial and so magnificently furnished this room seemed forlorn and neglected, out of place. The photographs of the colonel-commandants were faded. In romantic shakos and ill-fitting tunics, hands on sword hilts, they had all the sadness of the recent past. A few of the earlier ones wore whiskers. These had given place to heavy silken moustaches; these to ones the points of which had been greased. Towards the very end the moustaches had been clipped.

The leather of the settee was bullet-holed and torn. By the windows was a knee-deep pile of empty cartridge cases. The inkpot, still lying where it had fallen, had spread a wide black stain across the floor, visible here and there amidst the dust and wreckage. The glass was all gone from the window; the remnants of some blind or curtain chattered in the wind. With innocent but reproachful eyes the dead colonel-commandants surveyed the unimaginable untidiness of this room which in turn had belonged to each of them.

On the morning in question Colonel Moscardó was very busy but, on receiving this message, he crossed the courtyard and went into his office.

The chief of the Workers' Militia was still on the telephone. He informed Colonel Moscardó that he had his son in his power, and that unless the Alcazar were surrendered within ten minutes he would have him shot.

On receipt of the message Colonel Moscardó asked to speak to his son, so as to be certain that he was indeed in the hands of

79

the enemy. The young man was called to the telephone and for a few moments the father and son spoke together. Then the chief of the Workers' Militia took his place and repeated his threat. Colonel Moscardó at once told him that there could be no purpose in waiting for the ten minutes to elapse, as in no circumstances would he ever surrender the Alcazar, of which a sequence of unexpected events had placed him in charge.

The line was cleared.

A few minutes later Colonel Moscardó was again called to the telephone and informed that his son had been shot.

These are the bare facts. The following version of the conversation between Colonel Moscardó and his son is current everywhere in Spain. . . . I give it here, for what it may be worth. According to this version the boy asked what he should do. To which his father replied, "All you can do is to pray for us and to die for Spain."

To which the boy is reported to have said, "That is quite simple. Both I will do."

GEOFFREY MOSS *The Epic of the Alcazar*, 1937

GUARDIA CIVIL

The famous (and absurd) patent leather helmet, symbol of dictatorial authority, as much disliked by some Spaniards as their priests. But I have never felt so badly about the Guardia Civil since I gave one a lift. He was in splendidly shining uniform and carried a straw shopping basket with his groceries

HOLY BABIES

You can buy them in any size. Complete shops are devoted to holy subjects, from crucifixes to rainbow-coloured porcelain saints. It is to be expected in a country where holy relics were so industriously collected, sold, stolen and manufactured

FATHER OF THE CHURCH

Benign, bedecked with the flags of charity, in few countries has the priest been so honoured—and so hated. From the crusade against the infidel Moors to the Civil War, the Catholic Church has played the principal part in Spain's history, yet executing priests and burning churches have at times seemed national hobbies

Religion

Sancho, hemos topado con la iglesia.
"Sancho, we have come up against the church."

Don Quixote to Sancho Panza

Today this is quoted often and with feeling in Spain. Because the church supports the government and the government supports the church, religion is a real issue in a way it has ceased to be in most European countries. How strongly many Spaniards must feel about such an arrangement can be guessed from this scene which Kate O'Brien saw just before the outbreak of the Civil War.

SHADOW OF WAR

There is a very poor rough café on the corner of that street—the only café in Santillana. At this hour of the evening it was crowded at all its tables by smocked peasants, lorry-drivers and artisans in blue overalls. Some of them at a table outside the door were talking with unusual loudness, as if *at* somebody. A second's attention showed that they were talking, not ribaldly, but angrily about the little priest who continued to walk up and down, the width of the lane away from them. A big over-alled man, very powerful but also very weary-looking, stood up and shouted directly across to the priest, who turned, crossed over to him and asked if he wanted him. This angered everyone at the table, and some at other tables. No, no, they shouted, they didn't want him. Torrents of very passionate and no doubt very insulting Spanish broke from several men. The priest walked away, but as he had to catch his bus, could not walk out of their sight. They continued to discuss him furiously. I could not understand what they said, but they were not drunk, as a tourist new to Spain might have assumed. A Spaniard is almost never drunk. Politically most of them were probably anarcho-syndicalist, and this evening, perhaps because of some news in the papers or for some reason of local grievance, or merely because they were tired, this placidly pacing soutane, this imperturbable little symbol, got on their nerves more acutely

81

than was normal. They continued to rave and I thought the priest looked nervous now. He certainly didn't look pompous. If he was wearing the garb they hated, well, there was no help for that, his restrained uneasiness seemed to say—and perhaps indeed any minute there would be no help for him. As a looker-on I felt anxious, and said as much to a woman in the door of whose shop I was standing—but she smiled. As she did so, the big man and another young fellow, followed by a few less purposeful, rushed suddenly and really frighteningly at the priest and grabbed him. It looked very like being serious gangster-stuff, and I heard the priest say: "Well, what is the matter, my brothers?"

He said this furiously, like a man enraged. Nothing of the saint in his voice, no sweet oil on troubled waters. And yet he had the wit to say "my brothers", not—as a priest from habit might—"my sons".

The two big men were shaking him, and everyone was shouting. The priest shouted too. "Come on—what is it? No need to break my arm." Somehow, still in the clutches of the two, he managed to push his way through the rest of the crowd, ignoring them. "Say what you have to say. Come on." They marched him a few steps down the lane, still shouting. But he shouted too, and in a few seconds they let go of him, warming up to dialectics and needing the freedom of their hands. When they came to the end of the lane they turned as by one accord and came back, still arguing. Before they made another turn their Spanish gravity had returned. All three were masked and quiet—normal Spaniards. They spoke in turn now and wagged their heads slowly. Every few steps they halted, as Spaniards do when they walk and talk. Their faces were intensely serious. Then the priest's bus arrived. He had to skip down the lane to it. "*Adiós*," his two companions shouted, and he waved at them, his skirts flying. "*Adiós, padre*," all the rest of us shouted, and the two men went back to the café table.

Farewell Spain, 1937

It is the excesses of Spanish religious zeal which other Europeans have found sometimes incomprehensible, often horrifying.

THE JEWS EXPELLED

On the 30th March 1492 . . . the dread edict against the Jews went forth. Religious rancour had been inflamed to fever heat against these people, who were amongst the most enlightened and useful citizens of the State, and whose services to science, when the rest of Europe was sunk in darkness, make civilisation eternally their debtor. They were said to carry on in secret foul rites of human sacrifice, to defile the Christianity that most of them professed, and Isabel's zeal, prompted by the churchmen, was already climbing to the point afterwards reached by her great-grandson, Philip II, when he swore that, come what might, he would never be a king of heretic subjects.

By the 30th July 1492 not a professed Jew was to be left alive in Isabel's dominions. With cruel irony, in which Ferdinand's cynical greed is evident, the banished people were permitted to sell their property, yet forbidden to carry the money abroad with them. At least a quarter of a million of Spaniards of all ranks and ages, men, women, and children, ill or well, were driven forth, stripped of everything, to seek shelter in foreign lands. The decree was carried out with relentless ferocity, and the poor wretches, straggling through Spain to some place of safety, were an easy prey to plunder and maltreat. It was a saturnalia of robbery. The shipmasters extorted almost to the last ducat to carry the fugitives to Africa or elsewhere, and then, in numberless cases, cast their passengers overboard as soon as they were at sea. It was said that, in order to conceal their wealth, the Jews swallowed their precious gems, and hundreds were ripped up on the chance of discovering their riches. There was no attempt or pretence of mercy. The banishment was intended, not alone to remove Judaism as a creed from Spain— that might have been done without the horrible cruelty that ensued—but as a doom of death for all professing Jews; for Torquemada had, five years before, obtained a Bull from the Pope condemning to major excommunication the authorities of all Christian lands who failed to arrest and send back every fugitive Jew from Spain.

MARTIN HUME *Queens of Old Spain*, 1906

In 1560 Frampton came to Seville to reclaim the goods of a fellow merchant which had been confiscated by the Inquisition. Frampton himself was arrested, continuously interrogated, tortured and kept in prison for two years and four months. He was lucky to escape a life sentence in the galleys or burning, the fate of many heretics.

PRISONER OF THE INQUISITION

And forthwith I was plucked up again; and after a while let down again. And being put down well near dead, and very faint of this torment of the *stappado*, they asked me in particular, What other thing touching the church of Rome I believed not in? I told them, that I had conferred in all things in faith as it was taught in England. Then, said they, say on, what it is. I told them, that there could be no remission of sins bought for money, as was in Spain by the pope's bulls. But that all sins were forgiven only by the death of Christ. And that this doctrine was taught in England. Wherein I believed. What sayest thou of the confession? said Licentiado Gasco. I told them, that it was not necessary for salvation. Nor purgatory was there none; and holy water a ceremony not good for any thing. Then said the Licentiado Gasco, Truth it is, that thou mayest be saved without holy water, and with the death of Christ only thou mayest be saved. But with the ceremonies of the church thou mayest be saved the better. As if thou go barefoot on the ground, thou mayest go easier with a pair of shoes on thy feet, and the warmer. Even so likewise believing on the sacraments and ceremonies of the church, thou mayest be saved the better.

And the third time I was plucked up again, where I thought to have made an end of my life. . . .

Frampton's account from JOHN STRYPE
Annals of the Reformation

If the cult of relics seems less shocking, it is quite as astonishing. By the time the body of St Teresa was publicly exposed for the fifth time in 1750, about 150 years after her death, one complete arm and some fingers of the other hand, one foot, several ribs, her neck, part of her jaw, her heart and her left eye were missing.

RELIQUES AT THE ESCORIAL

Eleven entire bodies of saints; among which is that of a very little saint, who was one of the innocent children murdered by order of Herod.

One hundred and three heads, above twelve hundred arms and legs; the shoulder-blade of St Laurence, in a silver case, which is of such ancient workmanship, as sufficiently demonstrates the bone to be his. . . . Many of these arms and legs belonged to the two squadrons of saints who combatted under the banners of St Maurice and St Ursula.

We possess also a thigh of the glorious martyr St Laurence; it is entire, but the hair is toasted (singed), the holes which were made in it by the prongs which turned him on the gridiron, are very visible. One of this saint's feet; the toes are entire, though contracted: between two of them is a small cinder, which in the eye of piety shines like a carbuncle.

A silver statue of St Laurence, which weighs eighteen arrobas (of twenty-five pounds each) ornamented with gold, to the weight of eighteen pounds: he holds in his hand one of the very bars of the gridiron on which he was broiled. . . .

In order to protect the edifice from lightning, there are several reliques, especially some of St Laurence, its patron, in metal cases, inserted in the balls and crosses which are on the top of the towers.

Spanish account of 1773

The Escorial was the palace of Spain's most fanatical Catholic king, Philip II, built as a penance for the sacking of St Quintin, where the Spanish troops had burned a church dedicated to St Lawrence.

KING PHILIP AT WORK

King Philip sat working in the Escurial—the gigantic palace that he had built for himself, all of stone, far away, high up, amid the desolation of the rocky Guadarrama. He worked incessantly, as no monarch had ever worked before, controlling from his desk a vast empire—Spain and Portugal, half Italy, the Netherlands, the Western Indies. He had grown old and white-haired in his labours, but he worked on. Diseases had attacked him; he was tortured by the gout; his skin was cankered, he was the prey of a mysterious and terrible paralysis; but his hand moved over the paper from morning till night. He never emerged now. He had withdrawn into this inner room of his palace—a small room, hung with dark green tapestries— and there he reigned, secret, silent, indefatigable, dying. He had one distraction, and only one; sometimes he tottered through a low door into his oratory beyond, and kneeling, looked out, through an inner window, as it were from a box of an opera, into the enormous spaces of a church. It was the centre of his great building, half palace and half monastery, and there, operatic too in their vestments and their movements and their strange singings, the priests performed at the altar close below him, intent upon their holy work. Holy! But his work too was that; he too was labouring for the glory of God. Was he not God's chosen instrument? The divine inheritance was in his blood. His father, Charles the Fifth, had been welcomed into Heaven, when he died, by the Trinity; there could be no mistake about it; Titian had painted the scene. He also would be received in a similar glorious fashion; but not just yet. He must finish his earthly duties first. He must make peace with France, he must marry his daughter, he must conquer the Dutch, he must establish everywhere the supremacy of the Catholic Church. There was indeed a great deal still to do, and very little time to do it in—he hurried back to his table; and it must all be done by himself, with his own hand.

The study where Philip II worked at the Escorial is preserved much as it was in his day, with next to it his bedroom. When I saw them I shared the astonishment others have felt that the vast Spanish Empire should have been governed from these rooms which have the bareness of a monastery cell and lack even a cell's privacy because they are more like a corridor.
Philip II's task was too much for one man.

THE DEATH OF PHILIP THE SECOND

The news was quickly carried to Whitehall; it was also carried to the Escurial. King Philip's agony was coming to an end at last. The ravages of his dreadful diseases had overwhelmed him utterly; covered from head to foot with putrefying sores, he lay moribund in indescribable torment. His bed had been lifted into the oratory, so that his dying eyes might rest till the last moment on the high altar in the great church. He was surrounded by monks, priests, prayers, chantings, and holy relics. For fifty days and nights the extraordinary scene went on. He was dying as he had lived—in absolute piety. His conscience was clear; he had always done his duty; he had been infinitely industrious; he had existed solely for virtue and the glory of God. One thought alone troubled him: had he been remiss in the burning of heretics? He had burnt many, no doubt; but he might have burnt more. Was it because of this, perhaps, that he had not been quite as successful as he might have wished? It was certainly mysterious—he could not understand it—there seemed to be something wrong with his Empire—there was never enough money—the Dutch—the Queen of England . . . as he mused, a paper was brought in. It was the despatch from Ireland, announcing the victory of Tyrone. He sank back on his pillows, radiant; all was well, his prayers and his virtues had been rewarded, and the tide had turned at last. He dictated a letter to Tyrone of congratulation and encouragement. He promised immediate succour, he fore-

86

told the destruction of the heretics, and the ruin of the heretic Queen. A fifth Armada . . . he could dictate no more, and sank into a tortured stupor. When he awoke it was night, and there was singing at the altar below him; a sacred candle was lighted and put into his hand, the flame, as he clutched it closer and closer, casting lurid shadows upon his face: and so, in ecstasy and in torment, in absurdity and in greatness, happy, miserable, horrible, and holy, King Philip went off, to meet the Trinity.

LYTTON STRACHEY *Elizabeth and Essex*, 1928

In Philip II's reign came the Armada, not just a military exercise but a crusade.

THE HOLY ARMADA

Don Quixote, when he set out on his expedition, and forgot money and a change of linen, was not in a state of wilder exaltation than Catholic Europe at the sailing of the Armada. Every noble family in Spain had sent one or other of its sons to fight for Christ and Our Lady.

For three years the stream of prayer had been ascending from church, cathedral, or oratory. The King had emptied his treasury. The hidalgo and the tradesman had offered their contributions. The crusade against the Crescent itself had not kindled a more intense or more sacred enthusiasm. All pains were taken to make the expedition spiritually worthy of its purpose. No impure thing, specially no impure woman, was to approach the yards or ships. Swearing, quarrelling, gambling, were prohibited under terrible penalties. The galleons were named after the apostles and saints to whose charge they were committed, and every seaman and soldier confessed and communicated on going on board.

J. A. FROUDE
English Seamen in the Sixteenth Century, 1893–4

I find St Teresa of Avila a far more sympathetic fanatic. She travelled up and down Spain on mule and donkey, reforming Carmelite convents, in the last twenty years of her life founding seventeen of these without any apparent money. When the Inquisition heard that she had written her life it examined the book, but could find no fault.

One of my brothers was nearly my own age; and he it was whom I most loved, though I was very fond of them all, and they of me. He and I used to read Lives of Saints together. When I read of martyrdom undergone by the Saints for the love of God, it struck me that the vision of God was very cheaply purchased; and I had a great desire to die a martyr's death—not out of any love of Him of which I was conscious, but that I might most quickly attain to the fruition of those great joys of which I read that they were reserved in Heaven; and I used to discuss with my brother how we could become martyrs. We settled to go together to the country of the Moors, begging our way for the love of God, that we might be there beheaded; and our Lord, I believe, had given us courage enough, even at so tender an age, if we could have found the means to proceed; but our greatest difficulty seemed to be our father and mother. . . .

As soon as I saw it was impossible to go to any place where people would put me to death for the sake of God, my brother and I set about becoming hermits; and in an orchard belonging to the house we contrived, as well as we could, to build hermitages, by piling up small stones one on the other, which fell down immediately; and so it came to pass that we found no means of accomplishing our wish. Even now I have a feeling of devotion when I consider how God gave me in my early youth what I lost by my own fault. I gave alms as I could—and I could but little. I contrived to be alone, for the sake of saying my prayers—and they were many—especially the Rosary, to which my mother had a great devotion, and had made us also in this like herself. I used to delight exceedingly, when playing with other children, in building monasteries, as if we were nuns; and I think I wished to be a nun, though not so much as I did to be a martyr or a hermit.

St John of the Cross, a tiny man of five foot two, knew and worked with St Teresa. His mystical "love poems to God" are among the most beautiful of Spanish poetry.

EN UNA NOCHE OSCURA

Upon a gloomy night,
With all my cares to loving ardours flushed,
(O venture of delight!)
With nobody in sight
I went abroad when all the house was hushed.

A MEDIAEVAL SURVIVAL

According to mediaeval custom "Cabezudis", grotesque gnome-figures, are safeguards against evil spirits. This one, at a festival in Granada, is of a Moorish character

SAN FERMIN

Most famous of all Spanish fiestas, the feria at Seville excepted, is that of the large modern town of Pamplona in the Basque country where, on July 7th each year, the bulls charge through the streets while the men run in front. Each year some fail to keep ahead or to scramble to safety below the barriers

In safety, in disguise,
In darkness, up the secret stair I crept,
(O happy enterprise!)
Concealed from other eyes
When all my home at length in silence slept.

Upon that lucky night,
In secrecy, inscrutable to sight,
I went without discerning
And with no other light
Except for that which in my heart was burning.

It lit and led me through,
More certain than the light of noonday clear,
To where One waited near
Whose presence well I knew,
There, where no other presence might appear.

O Night that was my guide!
O Darkness dearer than the morning's pride,
O Night that joined the lover
To the beloved bride,
Transfiguring them each into the other!

Within my flowering breast,
Which only for himself entire I save,
He sank into his rest
And all my gifts I gave,
Lulled by the airs with which the cedars wave.

Over the ramparts fanned,
While the fresh wind was fluttering his tresses,
With his serenest hand
My neck he wounded, and
Suspended every sense in its caresses.

Lost to myself I stayed,
My face upon my lover having laid
From all endeavour ceasing:
And, all my cares releasing,
Threw them amongst the lilies there to fade.

Trans. Roy Campbell

Beside its long Catholic tradition and list of Saints,
Spain has an anti-clerical tradition. Alexandre Dumas,

author of *The Three Musketeers*, went to Spain with a party of friends in 1846, taking an African servant and six cases of rifles.

MONKS' EGGS

I asked our hostess for the first item, "a couple of boiled eggs." She understood my Spanish at once, but puzzled me by asking whether I would like a monk's couple or a layman's. "Surely 'a couple of eggs' means simply 'a couple of eggs'?" I learned that "a monk's couple" consists of three eggs, but "a couple of eggs for a layman" means two only. It seems that the monks enjoyed wide privileges before the revolution drove them from Spain.

Paris to Cadiz, 1846

In a remote corner of north-west Spain is the town of Santiago de Compostela, a centre of mediaeval pilgrimage second only to Rome. For here Saint James the Apostle is buried, though how exactly he got here seems uncertain. The pilgrims' way through Spain is a fascinating one to follow with its hostels and shrines. The converging routes from different parts of Europe met for this Spanish stretch and its small towns and villages must have once had a lively cosmopolitan flavour. In the sixteenth century an English doctor made his pilgrimage, starting at Paris.

DOCTOR ANDREW BOORDE'S PILGRIMAGE

I dyd mete with .ix. Englyshe and Skotyshe parsons goyng to saynt Compostell, a pylgrymage to saynt Iames. . . . And after that I went wyth them in theyr iurney thorow Fraunce, and so to Burdious & Byon; & than we entred into the baryn countrey of Byskay and Castyle, wher we coulde get no meate for money; yet wyth great honger we dyd come to Compostell, where we had plentye of meate and wyne; but in the retornyng thorow Spayn, for all the crafte of Physycke that I coulde do, they dyed, all by eatynge of frutes and drynkynge of water, the whych I dyd euer refrayne my selfe. And I assure all the worlde, that I had rather goe .v. times to Rome oute of Englond, than ons to Compostel. . . .

DR ANDREW BOORDE
The Fyrst Boke of the Introduction of Knowledge, 1542

Feast Day and Fiesta

I often find things said to be dead are alive and hearty.

VIOLET ALFORD

Spain seems to us today, in the words of the travel brochure, a land of fiestas. Mass entertainment and easy travel (not to mention Protestantism) have destroyed our own local feast days—though I wonder if they were ever quite as gay as the Spanish. Because Spain still has so many, all but the biggest keep their charm and simplicity. They always give me powerful doubts about whether we are really learning to organize our lives better. Going round Spain in September one year I remember feeling that every town and village was having, had just had, or was just about to have its fiesta. Perhaps the best of all was in a small town in Aragon.

I remember the fireworks on wires above the streets, and the dancing, and the drummer and piper at dawn who had been touring the town all night. And the feeling of a community all on holiday together, a feeling no social clubs or community centres can create in an English town. Most clearly I remember the tune which ran through the whole fiesta, and which had the gathering excitement of certain traditional tunes, so that each time it ended it seemed poised to break out with greater energy.

IN THIS WILD LAND

The tiny city of Jaca stands on its arid ridge, open to every wind. Until its eleven towers and encircling wall were pulled down, snow lay in its streets till May. Its people say the climate is now softened, so when the first Friday in May brings out the Procession of the Victory it marches through streets clear of slush. This is the first *Morisca* we meet in the land which gave birth to these complex performances. . . . Young men in the

91

costume of upper Aragon, but with hats entirely covered with flowers, and carrying guns, are the Labourers; *cabezudos* . . . run before them; robed priests and macebearers march with the town councillors and companies of armed young men. Their leader represents Count Aznar, a tenth-century ruler, and as his name denotes, a Navarrese of royal family. They march out to the Chapel of the Victory, line up and fire into the air. A man called the Moorish King falls, but there are now no Moorish troops and all the firing comes from one side. On this day great baskets of bread stand in the street for anyone to help himself. . . .

We return to Jaca for June 25th in a train crowded with *endemoniados*, the possessed, seeking a miracle. The previous afternoon the Romeros de la Confradia de Santa Orosia have arrived on foot, in the dirtiest of pilgrim cloaks, the greasiest of felt hats, accompanied by bearers of the Parish crosses, as dirty as themselves and more truculent. They have come from west of the Gallego river, for those living to the east have another destination. That evening the real fiesta breaks out, bands playing, *cabezudos* running, and the *ronda de la villa* in its bough-bedecked lorry with guitarists, players of the *bandurria* (the treble, metal-stringed guitar) and *Jota* singers, all rambling round the town in today's substitute for a long mule cart.

Next day the Church procession makes its *ronda de la villa*, wretched epileptics tightly packed beneath the *châsse* on which the reliquary is borne. They used to spend the night in the cathedral, which piteous vigil is now happily suppressed. Now the dancers ought to appear as they should have gone to meet the *romeria* the previous day, but frequently do not. A fine contrast they make to the ancient pilgrim garb in their gala dress, with scarves, stick in either hand, dancing, as they proceed, their *Paleotada*. Their musician plays a rustic three-holed pipe, covered with snake skin to keep its joints from parting, and marked by some enterprising hand Año 1402. In the crook of his left arm he carries that archaic stringed drum we have met before, which here on the southern slopes goes by the name of *Chicotén*.

At the mean and modern Templete a halt is made, the bishop appears on the balcony, two priests lift the lid of the reliquary, and the crowd surges below, staring, not at their venerated relics but at the endemoniados, hoping to see something worth waiting for. They have not long to wait. As the brocaded coverings are lifted a high, forced voice is lifted with them. "Now," says the crowd. "Now they are beginning."

A long, thin wail arises.

"Aï, aï Santa Orosia-a-a-a!" and a series of staccato screams

forced out in the most determinedly hysterical fashion imagin-
able, mingle with the foulest epithets.

"*Insultos*," says the crowd with satisfaction.

At the twentieth brocade the whole place is ringing with
shrieks, children adding their frightened wails, and the pilgrims
who order the procession are fighting to keep a space round the
miracle-seekers.

"She is tearing off her clothes," announces the crowd com-
placently.

Then the bishop steps forward to hold up to view a repulsive,
desiccated object, the size of a mummified cat, all bound about
with ancient ribbons and slung with medals. This he holds aloft
until the epileptics sink exhausted to the earth, and the crowd,
wearied, turns away to laugh and spit and push as though
coming out of a cinema. And the poor little remains of whatever
it is up there are reburied beneath a hundred brocades until
another year goes by.

VIOLET ALFORD *Pyrenean Festivals*, 1937

When I was in Valladolid at Holy Week I was lucky
enough to have a room in the Moderno, a hotel whose
name had dated, overlooking the town's central square,
gathering point of the various processions. Looking
down on these as they circled the town for hour after
hour and finally gathered for this or that climax,
filling the whole vast space below, I was astonished
most by the sheer size of the performance, and by the
weeks of organization it must require each year. Among
the regiments of hooded Ku-Klux-Klan figures, came
the religious tableaux, the lighter ones carried, the
heavier on wheels. There must have been at least thirty
of them, from individual saints to complete set-pieces
of the scenes of Easter.

A QUESTION OF PROPRIETY

Among the many processions of Holy week, there is one, of
the Virgin Mary and St John Baptist, which issues from the
church of St Juan, and makes the tour of the city, passing by
the cathedral. The procession left the church, and it began to
rain; the friars and their charge took refuge in the Franciscan
convent,—and the rain subsiding, the procession proceeded.
However, just as it reached the Plaza of the cathedral, a
tremendous storm burst overhead, and torrents of rain threatening to descend, the procession sought shelter in the cathedral.

93

Here it remained for some time; but the rain increased, and it began to grow dusk. The Virgin and John Baptist were in their best clothes, which the rain would have entirely spoiled; and besides, it would have shewn a want of respect to take them back to the church without the pomp usually attendant upon so important a procession. In this dilemma, it was resolved that the Virgin and John Baptist should remain in the cathedral all night; but now an unthought-of difficulty arose. Could the Virgin and John Baptist be left in the cathedral all night by themselves with any propriety? The canons were sent for, and the difficulty stated. One said, *"No es decente se quedase St Juan con ella."* "It is not decent to leave St John and her together." Another, a more jocular canon, quoted the well-known Spanish proverb, *"El fuego junto á la estopa llega el diablo, y sopla."* "When fire is put to the hemp, the devil comes and blows it." The result was, that a message was actually dispatched to the captain-general to request a guard; and a captain's guard, with torches, did accordingly keep watch upon the Virgin and John Baptist till morning.

HENRY D. INGLIS *Spain in 1830*

A SAINT OF THEIR OWN

In Avila, in these processions of Santa Teresa, there were charming survivals of popular naïveté, worthy of the Middle Ages. The Saint was too great, the crowds too large, for everything to go on in her own church; ten days before the feast she was borne to the Cathedral, where the image of the Virgin Mary was brought out from her chapel to welcome the pilgrim; and the two statues, one to the right and the other to the left of the high altar, presided over the ensuing Novena. When this was finished, another procession was formed to carry the Saint back to her own home; but such was her ascendancy in heaven as well as on earth, that the Virgin Mary herself could not forbear to accompany her parting guest at least half-way on the journey. At the appointed place, an open square where the eye could extend for some distance, the procession halted. Santa Teresa, who preceded (ecclesiastical etiquette requiring that the greatest shall come last), then turned completely round, and made three deep obeisances to the Queen of Heaven, who amid the delighted whispers and gratified vanity of the crowd actually made an obeisance in return, and then majestically moved away towards the Cathedral; whereupon the Saint resumed her homeward progress. So much for popular piety; but the pious also have their little human dissensions. At another hour there was another procession, by a rival confraternity, carrying a different newly bought image of Santa Teresa, in the style of Saint

94

Sulpice. And why? Because the regular Confraternity of Santa Teresa, whose property the old venerable image was, was said to be in the hands of rich men and ecclesiastics; and the artisans had seceded and formed a different confraternity of their own, with a modern pink-and-white image, plain painted stucco without silks or jewels, that they liked better.

GEORGE SANTAYANA *Persons and Places*, 1944

However much I tell myself that it is the hard dry uplands of Castile that I like, I fall quickly under the Andalusian influence as soon as I go there. And it is at Seville that I feel this most strongly. As in most Spanish towns, there are cold months at Seville and because the Spanish won't admit this and provide no heating except the *brasero*, a potentially lethal charcoal stove, I have been as cold here as anywhere in the world. But it is the heat at Seville which I remember and long for, the sort of engulfing heat which makes it unthinkable to move fast, and undesirable to do anything except wander in the shade between cafés. This, with the scent of the orange blossom, the glimpses through archways of cool Moorish courtyards and the sense that everywhere one is hearing or about to hear some song or phrase of music which has no place in Europe, make Seville unlike any other town I know.

I like Seville in midsummer when it is half-empty and half-alive for the heat. It is in spring that it comes alive with Holy Week, the greatest of all Spanish spectacles.

LOS PASOS AND LAS SAETAS

All Spain awakes at Eastertime to a sense of religious festival. The Passion of Jesus is, as it were, re-acted all over the country. In some districts and towns the scenes are acted by the people of the town; the judgement on Jesus proclaimed from the balcony of the Ayuntamiento, the disciples, the three Maries, the centurions and the Saviour, Saint Veronica and Saint John, walking to Calvary through the streets of their local town.

But for the most part the scenes are reconstructed by *pasos*, life-sized figures carved in wood, painted and grouped elaborately upon platforms which are carried on the shoulders of as many as forty men dressed in the habit of penitents. During the days of the Passion the processions reconstruct, as it were (among a people partially illiterate), the passage of Jesus through the streets and estranged populace to His trial, death, and burial. The carving of the figures themselves is of all degrees of elaboration, from the famous pasos of Seville, Valladolid, and Murcia, to the humble little local carvings of the villages. Sometimes the history of creation and pagan mythology are added to the story of Redemption. Sometimes the humble images of the village churches serve the purpose of the procession, which is the survival or renewal of the old mystery plays of the Church, now, as in medieval England, in the hands of the trade-guilds of the town and followed in procession by the confraternities of these guilds in the distinctive dress of each order.

Seville and Madrid set the standards of magnificence, but it is always of Seville that one hears all through Spain. "As in Seville," prints the tailor on his announcements for guild dresses. "You have seen the pasos of Seville?" ask the people of the little towns. . . .

As the groups of the Passion are carried through the towns and villages of Spain during Holy Week, short, flying songs greet them, supplying the dramatic reaction to the sculptured tragedy enacted in silence along the highway. To watch the spectacle of the processions and not to understand these songs, these *saetas* which greet and accompany them, is to go away with only an imperfect appreciation of the most popular religious festival in Spain. . . .

All traffic being stopped in the streets on Thursday until Sunday is past, the pasos repeat the incidents of the Passion in their due order and at recorded hours, and the action and speech, as it were, are supplied by these "arrows" of song, launched apparently into the air by spontaneous feelings of the crowd in the street. Part expressions of devotion, part wake-songs or dirges, part survival of acted scenes, intoned on high notes with a strangely Oriental music, the effect of these "dark grieving doves" circling the head of the Crucified, of the mourners and of the Lady of Sorrows, naïve and rude as these sometimes are in execution, can be deeply moving in their effect. . . .

One is to think of the darkened streets at midnight with the Paschal moon riding the clouds. The long black lines of waiting figures, the Cross with all the world's sorrow upon it, lit by the candles of the penitents in black hoods, advancing upon the night, cleaving the dark with its light like an opportunity. Suddenly upon the darkness flies a saeta to greet it:

> Lift up your eyes on high!
> Tell out with all your powers
> The thing which Jesus suffered
> In His grievous passion.

Or, more dramatic:

> "They are striking blows on Calvary.
> Magdalene, what does it mean?"
> "Ah, it is Jesus of Nazareth
> Whom they are nailing there."

Or again in swift action:

> Who will lend me a ladder
> That I may climb the Cross
> And draw the nails from the hands
> Of my father Jesus?

There are saetas for every development of the tragedy; for the betrayal and judgement, the supper, the scourging and humiliation; for the disciples and mourning women, and very many for the grief of the Lady of Sorrows who is carried alone through the streets in the last procession. Some of the latter are the most popular, and many of them poetic and touching. The preoccupation of so many with the embroidered mantle suggests ideas reaching into folklore, but to the women who send a saeta to greet the Virgin, the mantle means the work of women and what they have been able to afford for the Virgin's special hour. . . .

The pasos halt before the hospitals and there is one saeta . . . which I cannot refrain from repeating, though in literal English translation it loses much of its pathetic intensity.

> Open the window, Mother:
> The Brotherhood is passing.
> I am dying and I would see my Lord
> Go to His last agony,
> Oh! if I could die too when He does.

And for the prison:

> Ah, Lonely One, give me your hand!
> Here we are many brothers
>   without father or mother.

The processions have their interest as a spectacle, but the playing backwards and forwards of these saetas above their heads brings a deeper and more emotional quality into this festival, so popular among the Spanish people.

GERTRUDE BONE *Days in Old Spain*

Bullfighting is often a central fiesta attraction, and nowhere more so than at the Basque town of Pamplona.

97

Before the waiter brought the sherry the rocket that announced the fiesta went up in the square. It burst and there was a grey ball of smoke high up above the Theatre Gayarre, across on the other side of the plaza. The ball of smoke hung in the sky like a shrapnel burst, and as I watched, another rocket came up to it, trickling smoke in the bright sunlight. I saw the bright flash as it burst and another little cloud of smoke appeared. By the time the second rocket burst there were so many people in the arcade, that had been empty a minute before, that the waiter, holding the bottle high up over his head, could hardly get through the crowd to our table. People were coming into the square from all sides, and down the street we heard the pipes and the fifes and the drums coming. They were playing the *riau-riau* music, the pipes shrill and the drums pounding, and behind them came the men and boys dancing. When the fifers stopped they all crouched down in the street, and when the reed-pipes and the fifes shrilled, and the flat, dry hollow drums tapped it out again, they all went up in the air dancing. In the crowd you saw only the heads and shoulders of the dancers going up and down.

In the square a man, bent over, was playing on a reed-pipe, and a crowd of children were following him shouting, and pulling at his clothes. He came out of the square, the children following him, and piped them past the café and down a side-street. We saw his blank pockmarked face as he went by, piping, the children close behind him shouting and pulling at him.

ERNEST HEMINGWAY *The Sun also Rises*, 1927

SAN FERMÍN, 1943

The festival of San Fermín of 1943 had been the first great gathering at Pamplona since before the Civil War and people from all over Spain attended it. No *feria* in Spain possesses fiercer gusto than San Fermín. There is excitement in the air, and from early morning the crowds line the streets waiting for the *encierro* of the bulls, who will be sacrificed in the afternoon. The spectacle is awe-inspiring to Northerners, who are not accustomed to find themselves so near to fighting bulls. Once the rocket has been let off we hear in the distance the roar of the crowd which becomes louder and louder as the bulls race through the streets headed by the crowd of young men in white linen trousers, white hempen sandals with long red laces and a red handkerchief round the neck. The bulls dash like lightning through the streets, for every passage had been barricaded except the straight road towards the bull-ring. There is no chance of competing in speed with a fighting bull, for even the trained runners, who give themselves a generous handicap, find themselves in a few moments pressed by the racing bulls, and, as the animals approach the ring, the crowds of more timid runners conglomerate and there is pandemonium; for the bulls maddened by the shouting crowds stampede and charge over those who have fallen in the *mêlée* and gore those who block their way. They race on like an avalanche over the writhing mass of grovelling human beings.

That year I was told, there were a number of serious casualties and I can well believe it, for the spectacle at the entrance to the ring was blood-curdling. When the bulls dashed into the ring the crowd followed them, and then began a savage *kermesse* of charging bulls, and steers jangling their cow bells, and men using their coats as *capas* to *torear* the bulls, and when the steers had led away the fighting bulls the crowd began to dance the *jota* which, after the hair-raising *encierro*, becomes a war dance, and reminds me of *jotas* I have seen danced by mountaineers in Ansó and Jaca.

WALTER STARKIE *The Road to Santiago*, 1957

Christmas has been so thoroughly adopted by the English and turned into their own and only nation-wide fiesta that I am sometimes surprised to remember that other countries celebrate it too.

THE SPANISH CHRISTMAS

Christmas in Spain for the tourist is . . . often a little sad. The real celebration takes place only on Christmas Eve. It is a completely family affair, a Gargantuan *fiesta*, during which everyone stuffs himself with turkey and marzipan dainties. I remember in Toledo, one Christmas Eve, wandering round the town at ten in the evening. Even the bars were closed and silent. Houses and streets were wrapped in a dark grey mist.

But later the churches began to fill up for midnight Mass and the youths came out on the streets, armed with rattles and *zambombas*. The steady thumping of this species of sonorous, earthenware bellows and the grinding of the rattles continued till five in the morning. Christmas Day was a day of rest for those with heavy heads and queasy stomachs.

JOHN HAYCRAFT *Babel in Spain*

Compare the following two accounts, Captain Carleton's of about 1708, John Haycraft's of 1958.

CARNIVAL TIME

The week before Lent commences, commonly known by the name of Carnival Time, the whole city appears a perfect Bartholomew fair; the streets are crowded, and the houses empty; nor is it possible to pass along without some gambol or jack-pudding trick offered to you. Ink, water, and sometimes ordure, are sure to be hurled at your face or clothes; and if you appear concerned or angry, they rejoice at it, pleased the more. the more they displease; for all other resentment is at that time out of season, though at other times few in the world are fuller of resentment, or more captious.

The younger gentry, or Dons, to express their gallantry, carry about them egg-shells, filled with orange or other sweet water, which they cast at ladies in their coaches, or such other of the fair sex as they happen to meet in the streets. . . .

Yet when Ash-Wednesday comes, you will imagine them more unaccountable in their conduct, being then as much too excessive in all outward indications of humility and repentance. Here you shall meet one, bare-footed, with a cross on his shoulder, a burden rather fit for somewhat with four feet. and which his poor two are ready to sink under, yet the vain wretch bears and sweats, and sweats and bears, in hope of finding merit in an ass's labour.

Others you shall see naked to their waists, whipping themselves with scourges made for the purpose, till the blood follows every stroke; and no man need be at a loss to follow them by the very tracks of gore they shed in this frantic perambulation. Some who, from the thickness of their hides, or other impediments, have not power by their scourgings to fetch blood of themselves, are followed by surgeons with their lancets, who, at every turn, make use of them, to evince the extent of their patience and zeal by the smart of their folly. While others, mingling amour with devotion, take particular care to present themselves all macerated before the windows of their mistresses; and even in that condition, not satisfied with what they have barbarously done to themselves, they have their operators at hand, to evince their love by the number of their gashes and wounds; imagining the more blood they lose, the more love they shew, and the more they shall gain. These are generally devoto's of quality; though the tenet is universal, that he that is most bloody is most devout.

After these street-exercises, these ostentatious castigations, are over, these self-sacrificers repair to the great church, the bloodier the better; there they throw themselves in a condition too vile for the eye of female, before the image of the Virgin Mary; though I defy all their race of Fathers, and their infallible

Holy Father into the bargain, to produce any authority to fit it for belief, that she ever delighted in such sanguinary holocausts. . . .

When Good-Friday is come, they entertain it with the most profound show of reverence and religion, both in their streets and in their churches. In the last, particularly, they have contrived about twelve o'clock suddenly to darken them, so as to render them quite gloomy. This they do, to imitate the eclipse of the sun, which at that time happened. And to signify the rending of the veil of the temple, you are struck with a strange artificial noise at the very same instant.

But when Easter day appears, you find it in all respects with them a day of rejoicing . . . there is a visible satisfaction darts out at their eyes, which demonstrates their inward pleasure in being set free from the confinement of mind to the dissatisfaction of the body. Every person you now meet greets you with a Resurrexit Jesus. . . . And all sorts of the best music (which here indeed is the best in all Spain) proclaim an auspicious valediction to the departed season of superficial sorrow and stupid superstition.

CAPTAIN GEORGE CARLETON *Memoirs*

CARNIVAL, RONDA AND ROMERÍA

I went with a friend who was in deep mourning for his grandmother. On Sunday morning, after Mass, we followed the special band round from house to house. As it stopped before each door, troupes of masked figures sprang out, like gaily coloured birds from a conjurer's hat. Soon the streets were full of grotesque shapes, dancing over the cobble-stones to the music. A large bear pranced with a milkmaid gripped in his arms. A cat which might have come from Cheshire mewed at the gigantic, long-tailed mouse it held in its paws. A vast negress rocked a bundle which squalled like a child, but on closer inspection proved to be a small kid-goat, which stared up in terror from its swaddling clothes, and kicked lustily.

The sun shone and the great game was to discover the sex of the masqueraders. A hairy leg sticking out from under the bulk of an ostentatiously pregnant woman was observed with rapture and pursued by a multitude of shrieking Furies, until its owner managed to escape to a house where he might disguise himself better.

"*Es muy grossero!*" commented my friend with a delighted smile and the scraps of conversation which rose above the band's music were certainly fresh, rustic and amusingly bawdy.

"*Qué eres? Chico o chica?*" asked a clown, looking down at the open fly-buttons of a being with the globe of the world on its shoulders.

"*Nada sale—debes ser chica!*" resumed the clown.

A figure, disguised as a street vendor, approached us with a small box in which were a couple of white mice.

"*Tienes conejo?*" asked my friend, peering into the box, whereupon everyone within earshot bent their gaily garbed bodies with laughter.

"What a pity we can't stay for the dance," said my friend later. "You can imagine what it is like."

"I can," I said, a trifle sadly. But my friend was in mourning and he wanted to return to Toledo, where he had no relatives, and go to one there.

"Of course in a dance complications arise," he went on. "One never knows if one's dancing with a boy or a girl. Many a man's been most disappointed out in the fields with the girl of his choice!"

"Of course for the poor there was more gaiety before the war," said Doña Carmen. "But there are still the Romerías."

Early in the morning of March 17th, the road leading up to the Sierra was thronged. There were long queues at all the bus stops. Lorries, bedecked with streamers or decorated with beribboned bowers, in which huddled girls dressed in gipsy costume, started off with their loads of gay workmen and work-women.

The origins of the Romería are difficult to determine. Perhaps they were once the farewell to pilgrims to Rome, when half the town followed the travellers out to a church on the road where they celebrated a last Mass together.

Nowadays the middle and upper classes are usually absent. "Those who have *poca educactión* get unpleasantly drunk and do *barbaridades*," said Carolina, explaining why she certainly would not be there.

Most of the groups are friends, or consist of *rondas*, which are associations devoted to spending the sum of monthly member-ship fees on bibulous evening fiestas. These celebrations and those of the Romerías follow a simple pattern usual in Andalusia.

One night, some time before the Romería, I attended a *ronda* in company with a rich cloth merchant. The reunion was in honour of the merchant who had rallied the discouraged group at a previous rainy Romería. He had appeared suddenly out of the mist on a white horse and had led them up to the church of Santo Domingo, where all had eaten and drunk their wine in a state of determined *alegría* under a fine drizzle.

We sat out in a small patio which smelt of wet washing and

urine. In a corner, rice was cooking on a large stove and on the balcony the women of the house stood with babies in their arms, dim figures above the lights, looking down on us. A strange seriousness reigned. The members of the *ronda* were awkward having us in their midst. The cloth merchant, who was stout and loud voiced, got up and made short speeches, most of which ended with *"Viva Córdoba!"* As the wine began to circulate, the workmen relaxed and the clapping became feverish.

"You don't have wine in England, do you?" asked a serious boy next to me.

It was impossible to leave one's glass on the table for a moment without a clamour of protest, and draining was followed immediately by refilling. The cloth merchant's speeches became longer and more frenzied. A couple began dancing. Everyone cheered. Unused to such a vast quantity of wine, I had to go out to be sick and returned completely purged and quite sober.

"Fantastic! These English!" said my neighbour. "This one's drunk more than we but he's not affected at all!"

Then, suddenly, the climax passed and everyone began to talk listlessly in small groups. Food was announced and we shuffled to the front of the tavern. We sat munching our rice. Even the cloth merchant had to admit that he couldn't eat everything set on his plate.

"I have to get up at seven to load my lorry," said the boy next to me. But everyone, although quieter, was satisfied. The traditional rhythm of the exuberant orgy had been followed. *"Qué alegría!"* It would be a solace to think about when loading a lorry in the small hours or breaking stones in the heat of the day.

The Romerías are more satisfying than these small reunions because they embrace more people, because they are out in the country and they have the joy of recognised days of *fiesta*. They are the Spanish "bread and circuses" while the Carnival, because of the anonymity it allows, can be the expression of the Spanish Id.

The number of Romerías has increased considerably since the war. "It is to keep the people happy," remarked Manolo. And happy the people certainly seem. On March 17th we took a bus and drove up to within two miles of the shrine. Then we joined the long, ant-like procession and wound our way over the scrub-covered hills, till the solitary church came in sight. A father carried his youngest child, while the older ones trooped after their mother like baby ducklings. Workmen struggled under jars of wine, barrows were stacked perilously with picnic bundles, while four or five boys strummed guitars.

At the foot of the slope on which the church stands, a small town of stalls had been set up. Ice-cream was being scooped out of rusty-looking wells. Sweets and *turrón* lay on barrows in such profusion that one wondered how they would ever be sold. A seller of soft drinks had called his stall "Paris".

We found a place and had our picnic.

Thousands of people were sitting under the trees or up on the slopes. Down in the valley stood the decorated lorries. The competition for the most spectacular one had been held and the winners sported large placards suspended among the paper flowers, which announced the place they had gained. From the top of the slope we could see figures twirling like puppets, while the faint beat of palm on palm came up to us. A band from the circus in town came round and played. A shabby boy beat on the drums, a plump, spotty girl swelled as she blew the cornet.

After lunch we went down to the church. In front was a long bar, round which were grouped those of the *señoritos* who had decided to come. On the verandah, at the side of the building, one of the Holy Week brotherhoods, a *Cofradía*, were having lunch, looking like any Rotary Club; stout, elderly men chewed between sentences and people made speeches.

Outside the church a long queue was standing waiting to pass in front of the Virgin. The crutches of people who had been cured miraculously hung on one wall of the porch. Another was covered with small, framed paintings depicting various pilgrims who had been cured of stomach trouble. A smudgy man lay writhing on a bed while a nebulous Virgin extended a quieting hand.

We passed into the church which like so many others was gaudy with gilded wood and waxen figures. *"Qué bonita,"* said a lady in black who stood behind us. We bent our knees when our turn came and wandered back to the stalls once again. People were packing up to go home. The lorries were filling up for their picturesque procession back into town. Feet kicked up the dusty road.

The climax was past, and now everyone was cheerful but quiet. The rhythm followed at the meeting of the *ronda* had been completed. This cycle of rhapsodic energy, succeeded by exhaustion and indifference, can be noted not only in reunions but also in the way Spaniards embrace ideas or in the ebb and flow of their expressions of friendship. It can be observed also in the contrasting liveliness and dullness of Spanish town life. ... To the unlucky traveller the Spaniard is boring and melancholy; to the lucky one he is gay and exhilarating. This fluctuation is perhaps another part of the "enigma" of which foreign visitors are so often conscious in Spain—which creates an uncertainty of what the Spaniard is at any given moment, or of what he is really capable.

JOHN HAYCRAFT *Babel in Spain*

THE GYPSY DANCE

From the smart cafés of Madrid and Barcelona to the now equally smart caves of Granada, the dancing of the Spanish Gypsies can be seen all over Spain. If you're unlucky it will be expensive and second rate. At its best it's the most exciting of all dancing

MASTER AND MAN

*Across the Plaza de España rides Don Quixote on
Rozinante and Sancho Panza follows on his ass, just as
one has always imagined them riding across the landscape
of La Mancha. Behind rise Madrid's new skyscrapers*

With Pen and Brush

Towards 1766 two Franciscan friars, Fray Pedro and Fray Rafael Mohedano, sat down to write the history of Spanish literature. It was the age of long books and the good friars wished to do the job thoroughly. When at last they died, after twenty-five years of continuous work, they had finished ten volumes, bringing their history down to the year A.D. 65.

GERALD BRENAN

ON THE MARTYRDOM OF F. GARCÍA LORCA

> Not only did he lose his life
> By shots assassinated:
> But with a hatchet and a knife
> Was after that—translated.

ROY CAMPBELL

After such warnings perhaps it would have been better to miss out this section. Spanish literature is vast and, apart from Cervantes, little known in England. And it should no doubt be read in the original. Just the same there are good as well as bad translations, and the best can tempt one further. As for Spanish painting, like all painting it should be looked at, not written about.

THE WHOLE MAN

It seems that Spain is the only part of the world in which the art of painting has been continuously cultivated since the prehistoric cave-dwelling days. Painting, as the soul's endeavour to capture and retain movement, is a characteristically Spanish art. In painting the artist, as a spectator and a re-creator of what he sees, grants permanence to the fleeting instant of life; body and spirit are caught in their unity, expressing each other in perfect unison. This whole-human aspiration of the art of painting explains why it should be the favourite art of Spain. It also explains a number of features in the history of Spanish

105

painting: the poverty of its landscapes, the richness of its portraits, the scarcity of its nudes, the homely and earthly atmosphere of religious subjects—all features which suggest direct observation of human life as it actually is. Painting, moreover, is a natural expression in a people of spectators. Generations of lookers-on may have drunk in life so that a Velázquez or a Goya becomes exhilarated by it. In her great pictures, Spain has given the world a crowd of human beings whom we remember individually, and every one of whom stands in our memory with that spring-like vitality which the Spanish genius brings out and cherishes in individual man.

This whole-human conception of man is symbolized also—as well as exemplified—in the concrete human characters Spain has given to world literature. I take it that the four biggest characters of literature are Don Quixote, Hamlet, Don Juan, and Faust. Of the four, two are Spanish; and, though universal, thoroughly Spanish; for both, each in his way, incarnate the Spanish tendency to put men above things and to force things to accept the will of man. Don Quixote has a reality of his own and he will not tolerate "that thing" outside, which calls itself reality, to stand in his way. When he has made up his mind that the windmills are giants, giants they are to be. Cervantes, of course, pokes fun at the conflict thus created; but he himself, by his Quixotic life as a slave in Algiers, proved to be as Quixotic as Don Quixote himself. It is thanks to the Quixotic spirit of Columbus that America was discovered; and thanks to the Quixotic spirit of Cortés, Pizzaro, Quesada, and the rest, that it became European. . . .

As for Don Juan, he has no reality in his head, for his head is empty. Don Juan is a force of nature, the whole man in revolution against society; the last spurt of the anarchist volcano as the forces, rules, laws, and standards of modern society assert themselves in the Europe of Charles V and Philip II, of Henry VIII and Elizabeth I. Don Juan respects no law, whether human or divine. His whim or his desire are his only motive power. He seduces women and leaves them as soon as seduced, for he must hurry to the next. Naturally enough, Don Juan became immensely popular; for what could be more delightful for women than a man ready to make love a whole-time job? That he was apt to change his partner was sad enough for the outgoing one, but not for the others. And then, since women, like heaven, suffer themselves to be taken by force, Don Juan answered to deep human impulses and impersonated them to perfection. Don Juan is thus an apt symbol of this Spanish way I am endeavouring to outline: no one pays more attention to women than he does; no one, however, treats them worse. But Don Juan is symbolic only of one aspect of the Spanish way; which can only be fully understood by bearing in mind the other symbol: Don Quixote.

The outstanding vigour of these two Spanish symbols strikes the mind at once. Turn your eyes for a while to other Europeans of the spirit—Hamlet, Faust, Ivan Karamazov; and you will perceive the contrast between these wondering, hesitating, suffering souls, lingering in a mental purgatory, *depending* on and expecting some outside help that never comes—and the two Spaniards, overflowing with their own selves, free and independent from any outside help or even collaboration, imprinting on the world outside the seal of their rebellious personalities.

SALVADOR DE MADARIAGA *Essays with a Purpose*, 1954

Don Juan's inventor was Tirso de Molina (1583–1648), a playwright of Spain's golden age, whose works totalled about 400 dramas.

Courage was Don Juan's one great quality. In the graveyard he meets the statue of the dead Don Gonzalo, whom he murdered. Tirso de Molina probably got the idea for this scene from the old custom in parts of Spain of visiting graveyards on All Souls' Night to pray for the dead, a custom which came to include toasting the dead and inviting them to eat, but what is really Spanish about it is the admiration it implies for the personal courage, even of such a clearly deplorable character, in the face of defeat and death.

THE PENALTY

At the sepulchre of Don Gonzalo de Ulloa.

DON JUAN. Who comes?
DON GONZALO. It is I!
CATALINON. Oh, I am dead already—here comes our Dead Man!
DON GONZALO. Yes, I am dead. It is my natural state now;
No man could live with such a wound as this.
I hardly thought that you would keep your word
Since your one pleasure is deception, sir!
DON JUAN. Surely you did not think I am a coward?
DON GONZALO. I did . . . because you ran away that night
On which you put my age to death.
DON JUAN. I fled to escape being known
And not for any fear: tonight you'll find me
Ready for any danger. . . . Tell me swiftly
Your will.
DON GONZALO. Merely that I've invited you to dine.

CATALINON. Excuse us from your table, sir, tonight.
Your food is cold, and I observe no kitchen
To heat it in.
DON JUAN. Be quiet! Then let us dine!
DON GONZALO. To dine, we'll have to lift this burial slab.
DON JUAN. I'll tear the tombstones up for seats, if need be.
DON GONZALO. You are no coward; you are brave indeed!
DON JUAN. It is not that I'm more than other men,
But that I rule my flesh with resolution.
CATALINON. Pst! Master, see, the table's made of gold!
DON GONZALO. Be seated, guests!
DON JUAN. I find no chairs to sit on.
CATALINON. Here come his two black footmen, bearing chairs.
  Two black-shrouded figures, bearing chairs, come in.
DON GONZALO. Sit down!
CATALINON. I, sir—lunched quite late, sir.
DON GONZALO. Don't answer back!
CATALINON. Yes, I won't answer back, sir.
(*Aside.*) Now may God bring me from this place alive;
I see it isn't pleasant, being dead.
What dish is this, sir?
DON GONZALO. A dish of scorpions.
CATALINON. What a dainty dish!
DON GONZALO. This is the favourite food we dead men eat—
Why don't you eat?
DON JUAN. I'll eat your food
If you serve all the asps that hell contains.
DON GONZALO. And now I'll have them sing a song for you.
CATALINON. What kind of wine do dead men drink?
DON GONZALO. Taste and see.
CATALINON. A bitter drink of gall and vinegar.
DON GONZALO. It is the only wine our presses give.
              Song; without.
        Behold the souls whom God has judged
            Beyond the crimes of men:
        They'll see no rest until they've paid
            Again and yet again.
CATALINON. I find an evil meaning in that song.
It's sung at us.
DON JUAN. A living fire from hell
Clutches my breast.
              Song: continued.
        Though man walk big about the earth
            It is not fitting he should say
        "I have a long time yet to live,"
            Because the living die each day.
DON JUAN. Now that we've dined, let's put the burial slab

Back where we found it.

DON GONZALO. Give me your hand, you do not fear to give me
Your hand?

DON JUAN. Why must you always ask me if I fear?
You burn me! Do not burn me with your fire!

DON GONZALO. This is a foretaste of the fire you'll know.
The miracles of God are manifest
And are past finding out as they are many.
Witness it, that you pay now for your crimes
At a slain man's hands—the man you murdered;
The Living Dead that pays you in this fashion
Beyond the knowledge of recorded time.
There is no stranger thing than God's revenge.
For your strange sins you pay in a strange way!

DON JUAN. Alas, a searing fire flows through my body.
From you—your hand crushes my aching fingers
Until the blood streams from their bursting ends.
You monstrous hell-thing,
Take this in the wound I gave you!
It only wounds the unwounded air with blows.
No more, good God! No more!
I swear I did not touch your daughter, sir—
You came before I played the game quite through!

DON GONZALO. That will not save you, in your soul you did.

DON JUAN. Let me go but a little while. . . .
I will come back . . . my word, you know, is good. . . .
I am Don Juan Tenorio . . .
A gentleman of the King's court. . . .
I will come back. . . .
As you're a Christian, let me die confessed.

DON GONZALO. Upon the threshold of eternity
It is too late now for a good resolve.

DON JUAN. God, how I burn! God, how the flames melt through
        me!
They pour like water, yet they spread like fire!
I die. (*Falls dead.*)

El Burlador de Sevilla, trans. Harry Kemp

From Mozart to Byron, Pushkin to Shaw, later writers
and musicians have used the Don Juan story. Best
known in Spain is *Don Juan Tenorio* by Zorilla, a
nineteenth-century playwright. I think this is spoilt
when Don Juan is saved by the pure love of Doña
Inés, even though, as V. S. Pritchett says, he "is
still shouting about his honour and obviously going to
be very troublesome in heaven".

D. JUAN TENORIO

There is one [play] which must on no account be missed; it is Zorilla's *D. Juan Tenorio*, always played in every Spanish town where there is a theatre on All Saints Day, and always attended by vast crowds as if it were a religious ceremony. The story is Don Juan, taken from the old Spanish plays. As drama the piece may or may not be interesting; but the enthusiasm of the audience is magnificent. Every man, woman, and child knows some passage by heart, and when that passage arrives all who know it repeat it after the actor. The culminating point is approached in the lines:

> *La barca del pescador*
> *que espera cantando el dia,*
> *no es cierto, paloma mia,*
> *que están respirando amor?*

soon after which Da. Ana falls into Don Juan's arms.

The effect is very curious, and reminds one of prayers at Harrow, when the shell was taken by the French master and used to gabble out the responses at the wrong places, causing blasphemous confusion. In the case of the Spanish audience, however, the motive is something approaching religious exaltation. The God is upon them. They are drunk with the sound of their gorgeous Castilian. They obey the impulse which makes the Italians sing at the opera.

ROYALL TYLER *Spain: Her Life and Arts*, 1909

HERE LIVES ...

The famous moment when Don Juan describes how he nails up his truculent notice on the door of his house, saying: "Here lives Don Juan Tenorio and if any man wants anything of him . . ." has become a proverbial satire of Spanish defiance. Don Juan's is an act which, in some form or other, every Spaniard dreams of performing, and in fact in his inner life is doing all the time. He is asserting the exclusive, dramatic rights of the human ego—myself before all other selves, unrepentantly.

V. S. PRITCHETT *The Spanish Temper*

If Cervantes' *Don Quixote* was the original of the modern novel, as we understand it, an anonymous story of fifty years earlier was the first novel of the picaresque, with a rogue for its hero. He is a thieving boy, who passes from master to master, each meaner than the last. His fantastic adventures make Spain of the sixteenth century as alive to me as Spain today.

BLIND MAN'S BOY

When we were staying at an inn in Escalona, a town belonging to the duke of that name, my master gave me a piece of sausage to roast. Once the sausage was dripping and he had eaten some bread dipped in its fat, he took a penny from his purse and sent me to the inn for wine. Now the devil presented me with the opportunity, and opportunity, as they say, makes the thief. There happened to be a little turnip beside the fire, a poor thing that must have been thrown out as unfit for the pot. Now as he and I were alone in the room and my appetite had been aroused by the smell of the sausage—which I knew was all I was to enjoy of it—without a thought for the consequences I threw aside all my fear in order to get my desire. So when the blind man was extracting the money from his purse I seized the sausage and rapidly put the aforementioned turnip on the spit in its place. After giving me the money for the wine my master took it and began to turn it in front of the fire, setting out to roast this object that was so miserable as to have escaped being boiled. I went for the wine and quickly gobbled the sausage on my way, and when I returned I found that old sinner holding the turnip between two slices of bread. Not having touched it he had not discovered what it was. But when he took the slices and put his teeth into them, expecting to bite into the sausage, he felt the sudden chill of the cold turnip. His expression changed and he shouted out:

"What's this, Lázarillo?"

"God bless me," I replied, "you can't accuse me of anything! Haven't I just been out for the wine? Somebody must have come in and done it for a joke."

"No, no, that's impossible," he said. "I didn't put the spit down for a second."

I swore again and again that I was innocent of that swap or substitution. But it was no use. Nothing escaped the sharp wits of that accursed blind man. He got up, seized me by the head and started to smell me, and like a good hunting dog he must have caught the scent. But to make more certain, being in a great fury, he grasped hold of me, opened my mouth to more than its usual extent and somewhat rashly stuck in his nose, which was long and pointed, and at that moment on account of his anger, quite nine inches longer than usual. So the tip stuck in my gullet. Then, what with my terror, and the short time since I had swallowed the sausage—the wretched thing had not yet settled in my stomach—and the ill-timed probing

of that enormous nose into the bargain, which half choked me—
what with all these things together my deed and greed were
revealed and the property was returned to its owner. Before
the wretched man could extract his trunk from my mouth my
stomach was so upset that it gave up the booty. His nose and that
unfortunate ill-chewed sausage left my mouth at the same time.

Oh God, I wish I had been buried at that moment, for I
was as good as dead. That wicked old man was so furious that
I do not think he would have left me alive if some people had not
been roused by the noise. They pulled me away from him, leaving
his hands full of the few hairs remaining to me. My face was
scratched and my throat torn. And the latter certainly deserved
it, since its wickedness was the cause of all my troubles. . . .

At that moment however I was struck by my own cowardly
weakness and cursed myself for not having bitten off his nose,
since I had had such a good chance and had been half way to it.
I need only have closed my teeth and the deed would have been
done. Then since it belonged to that wicked old man perhaps my
stomach would have retained it better than it did the sausage.

La Vida de Lázarillo de Tormes, 1554
Trans. J. M. Cohen

Spanish ballads were sung and repeated, half-forgotten
and added to all over Spain for many hundreds of
years until the time of Ferdinand and Isabel when,
much as English folk-song has been this century, they
were discovered, collected and written down. Of them
all, I find Lord Arnaldos the most mysterious and
exciting, and the fifteenth-century original loses nothing
in Flecker's translation.

LORD ARNALDOS

The strangest of adventures
That happen by the sea,
Befell to Lord Arnaldos
On the Evening of Saint John;
For he was out a-hunting—
A huntsman bold was he!—
When he beheld a little ship
And close to land was she.
Her cords were all of silver,
Her sails of cramasy;
And he who sailed the little ship
Was singing at the helm;

A NATIONAL PROPENSITY

If there isn't a live animal with horns then some horns will do. Football may be a rival entertainment for adults but it seems no substitute for Spanish children's imaginations

SEMANA SANTA

Through the dark streets of Vallodolid go the endless processions of
Holy Week, troop after troop of hooded figures, and then the pasos,
too many to count, outdoing each other in splendour and drama

COME TO GUADALAJARA

*For the opening fiesta of the new bullring—La más Cómoda
de España. It's only fifty kilometres from Madrid. There
will be fine bulls and these are the* toreros *who will fight them*

The waves stood still to hear him,
The wind was soft and low;
The fish who dwell in darkness
Ascended through the sea,
And all the birds in heaven
Flew down to his mast-tree.
Then spake the Lord Arnaldos,—
(Well shall you hear his words!)
"Tell me, for God's sake, sailor,
What song may that song be?"
The sailor spake in answer,
And answer thus made he:
"I only tell the song to those
Who sail away with me."

Lame, short-sighted and quarrelsome, Quevedo is a phenomenon of Spanish literature. His writing, in all forms of prose and verse, was mainly satirical, and the four years he spent in prison late in his life were probably because he was the suspected author of some insulting verses found by Philip IV in his napkin.

TO A NOSE

There was a man well fastened to a nose—
A nose superlative did he escort;
An executioner or scribe, in short,
A sword well barbed and sharp against its foes.
It was a sundial badly out of pose,
It was a musing alchemist's retort,
An elephant with trunk upraised in sport,
More nose than Roman Ovid did expose,
It was a fighting galley's pointed beak,
It was a pyramid on Egypt's pate,
Twelve tribes of noses in one nose sublime,
An infinite nose of noses, so to speak,
Very much of a nose it was, a nose so great
That in the face of Annas 'twere a crime.

FRANCISCO DE QUEVEDO Y VILLEGAS (1580–1645)
Trans. W. H. Burnham

The wolf who will not exchange the freedom and hunger of the forest for food and security is a very Spanish theme. The author of the following was an eighteenth-century fabulist.

113

THE WOLF AND THE DOG

A prowling wolf, whose shaggy skin
(So strict the watch of dogs had been)
Hid little but his bones,
Once met a mastiff dog astray;
A prouder, fatter, sleeker Tray
No human mortal owns.
Sir Wolf in famished plight,
Would fain have made a ration
Upon his fat relation;
But then he first must fight;
And well the dog seemed able
To save from wolfish table
His carcass snug and tight.
So, then in civil conversation,
The wolf expressed his admiration
Of Tray's fine case. Said Tray, politely,
"Yourself, good Sir, may be as sightly:
Quit but the woods, advised by me;
For all your fellows here, I see,
Are shabby wretches, lean, and gaunt,
Belike to die of haggard want;
With such a pack, of course, it follows
One fights for every bit he swallows.
Come, then, with me, and share
On equal terms our princely fare."
"But what, with you,
Has one to do?"
Inquires the wolf. "Light work indeed,"
Replies the dog; "you only need
To bark a little, now and then,
To chase off duns and beggar-men,—
To fawn on friends that come or go forth,
Your master please, and so forth;
For which you have to eat
All sorts of well cooked meat,—
Cold pullets, pigeons, savoury messes,—
Besides unnumbered fond caresses."—
The wolf, by force of appetite,
Accepts the terms outright,
Tears glistening in his eyes.
But, faring on, he spies
A galled spot on the mastiff's neck.
"What's that?" he cries. "O, nothing but a speck."
"A speck?" "Ay, ay, 'tis not enough to pain me;
Perhaps the collar's mark by which they chain me."

"Chain,—chain you? What, run you not, then,
Just where you please, and when?"
"Not always, Sir; but what of that?
Enough for me, to spoil your fat."
"It ought to be a precious price
Which could to servile chains entice;
For me, I'll shun them, while I've wit."
So ran Sir Wolf, and runneth yet.

FELIX MARÍA DE SAMANIEGO (1745–1801)

Sooner or later the squeamish, or those who prefer not
to see death as a permanent and integral part of life,
are not going to like Spain. It is fully integrated into
Spanish thought and behaviour in a way which sometimes gives our escapist habits of mind the flavour of
the nursery. Spanish poetry is preoccupied with death.
Bécquer, who only published one book of poems,
himself died of consumption at the age of 34. He seems
now the greatest of Spanish nineteenth-century poets.

RIMA LXXVIII

They closed her eyes
That were still open;
They hid her face
With a white linen,
And, some sobbing
Others in silence,
From the sad bedroom
All came away.

The nightlight in a dish
Burned on the floor;
It threw on the wall
The bed's shadow,
And in that shadow
One saw sometime
Drawn in sharp line
The body's shape.

The dawn appeared.
At its first whiteness
With its thousand noises
The town awoke.
Before that contrast

115

Of light and darkness,
Of life and strangeness
I thought a moment.
My God, how lonely
The dead are!

On the shoulders of men
To church they bore her,
And in a chapel
They left her bier.
Here they surrounded
Her pale body
With yellow candles
And black stuffs.

At the last stroke
Of the ringing for the Souls,
An old crone finished
Her last prayers.
She crossed the narrow nave,
The doors moaned,
And the holy place
Remained deserted.

From a clock one heard
The measured ticking,
And from a candle
The guttering.
All things there
Were so dark and mournful,
So cold and rigid,
That I thought a moment:
My God, how lonely
The dead are!

From the high belfry
The tongue of iron
Clanged, giving out
A last farewell.
Crêpe on their clothes,
Her friends and kindred
Passed in a line
In homage to her.

In the last vault
Dark and narrow,
The pickaxe opened

A niche at one end;
They laid her away there.
Soon they bricked the place up,
And with a gesture
Bade grief farewell.

Pickaxe on shoulder
The gravedigger,
Singing between his teeth,
Passed out of sight.
The night came down,
It was all silent.
Alone in the darkness
I thought a moment,—
My God, how lonely
The dead are!

In the dark nights
Of bitter winter,
When the wind makes
The rafter creak,
When the violent rain
Lashes the windows,
Lonely I remember
That poor girl.

There falls the rain
With its noise eternal,
There the northwind
Fights with the rain.
Stretched in the hollow
Of the damp bricks,
Perhaps her bones
Freeze with the cold.

Does the dust return to dust?
Does the soul fly to heaven?
Or is all vile matter,
Rottenness, filthiness?
I know not, but
There is something—something—
Something which gives me
Loathing, terror,—
To leave the dead
So alone, so wretched.

GUSTAVO ADOLFO BÉCQUER (1836–70),
trans. John Masefield

117

An eighteenth-century English traveller saw this curtain-raiser.

A FARCE OF 1773

It is entitled *The Hog of St Anthony*. The dramatis personae are, a Husband, his Wife, a Constable, a Sacristan, and a Sow-gelder.

The husband enters pensively, and in a soliloquy declares, that he suspects his wife's having a criminal intercourse with the Sacristan.

He surprises them conversing together; the sacristan walks off, and the husband beats the wife till she confesses, that the sacristan told her he loved her. The husband tells her he is obliged to go to a distant village, where he will remain all night, but intends to go only to his neighbour's house, in order to watch her.

Soon after his departure she apprises the sacristan of it, who comes for admittance, counterfeiting the mewing of a cat. He tells her, that he is at her feet attending her commands, "From age to age, for ever and ever, amen."

She advises him to act cautiously, because her husband was but just gone, and might soon return. He answers, that his head-piece will find a remedy for every thing, and that she may make him pass for St Anthony's hog. In the mean time, the husband knocks at the door, and the wife orders the sacristan to get into the hog-sty. The husband calls to his wife to open the door, and she tells him to wait till she has put on her shift: she then lets him in. He accuses her of changing colour, fastens the door, and declares he will search the house. The wife implores the assistance of the Virgin Mary, and vows to offer her a little silver sacristan, if she delivers her out of this scrape. The husband searches every where, and sees something move in the hog-sty. His wife tells him it is St Anthony's hog that was brought there the day before, because it spoiled the garden, and that she had fastened it with a rope. The sacristan runs on all four, with a hog's head fastened over his own. The husband, who feigns to mistake him for a real hog, asks his wife whether it is gelt? She answers, that to her certain know-ledge it is not. The sow-gelder passes by, and the husband goes out to call him in. The sacristan says, "thou devil of a woman, what shall I do, if they take away my appendages?" She answers, "Heaven will provide against it." The husband goes to fetch a cord to tie its feet: in the mean time, the sacristan swears, that he will drink the blood of the sow-gelder if he stirs. This poor fellow cries out, "libra me domine." The husband returns, and says, "I will disarm this hog that wanted to arm me:" he throws a noose over him; the sacristan struggles, and they fight. The constable hearing the noise, breaks open the door, and separates them, which concludes this ingenious and elegant entertainment.

RICHARD TWISS *Travels through Portugal and Spain*, 1773

The censor has overshadowed Spanish literature from the time of the Inquisition to today.

AN AUTHOR'S TROUBLES, 1830

A priest, with whom I was acquainted in Madrid, telling me one day, that he had thoughts of going to London or Paris, to print an English and Spanish Grammar, and a German and Spanish Grammar, which he had written; I asked him why he did not print them in Madrid, since they were intended for the use of his own countrymen,—especially as they could contain nothing political? His answer was, that nothing was so difficult as to obtain a licence to publish a book, even although it contained no allusion to politics; and "the better the book," said he, "the more difficult it is to obtain a licence, and the more dangerous to publish; because the Government does not wish to encourage writing, or even thinking, upon any subject: and the publication of a good book sets men a-thinking."

HENRY D. INGLIS *Spain in 1830*

1957

Like most groups of young Spanish intellectuals, they made a point of hating the government, in this case because of the censorship.

"*Mandan los muertos*," said Tomás one day, quoting a recent speech by a leader of the Falange. "Do the dead command in England?" he asked me.

"To a limited extent."

"Well, here they're the only ones who command!"

"Franco, though, will never die," said Antonio. "He'll go on and on, lose all his hair, celebrate his hundredth birthday—and we'll be in our graves with many a line written but none of it published."

"There must be thousands of novels, though, stacked away in a drawer while their authors wait patiently for the end of the regime," said Ricardo seriously.

JOHN HAYCRAFT *Babel in Spain*

After Cervantes, Lorca is today probably the best known Spanish writer outside Spain. He lived in Granada and was inspired by the folk-song and traditions of Andalusia. He was still only 37 when he was shot by the Fascists at the start of the Civil War.

PRECIOSA AND THE WIND

Beating upon the moon of parchment
Preciosa with her tambourine
Comes down by an amphibious path
Of laurel shade and crystal sheen.
The silence bare of any star,
Scared by the jangled sound she rings,
Falls where the deep sound of the ocean
Starry with fish, resounds and sings.
Amongst the peaks of the sierra
Slumber the coast-guard carbineers
Keeping a watch upon the towers
Where English folk have lived for years.
Beating on her moon of parchment,
Preciosa comes with rhythmic fall;
To see her come the rude wind rises,
The wind that does not sleep at all.
A huge Saint Christopher stark naked
Full of celestial tongues of air,
He looks upon the girl, and plays
On a sweet pipe that isn't there.
"Allow me, girl, to lift your skirt
And let me see you plain and clear.
Open to my ancient fingers
The blue rose of your beauty, dear!"

Preciosa flings away her tambour,
And runs, and runs, and does not tire
And the Big-Man-Wind pursues her
With a burning sword of fire.

The sea has puckered up its rumour,
All pale as death the olives grow.
The shrill flutes of the shadows sing.
So does the smooth gong of the snow.

Preciosa run! or the green wind
Will surely have you by the hair!
Run, Preciosa! run like mad!
Look out! He nearly got you there!

IN THE WINGS

It is nearly five o'clock and the toreros are waiting for the parade which will start another bullfight, this one in Palma, Maiorca. In a moment the trumpets will sound

PLACING THE BANDERILLAS

Second and most elegant phase of the modern bullfight. Three pairs of these darts with coloured paper frills are placed in the bull's neck, sometimes by the matador, sometimes by his banderilleros. Till recently there were explosive ones for cowardly bulls

The satyr of the setting stars
With all his glittering tongues of air.

Preciosa, terrified to death,
Runs into the first house she sees,
Where high above the lofty pines,
The English Consul lives at ease.

Alarmed to hear her piercing screams
Come rushing down three carbineers
With their black cloaks hugged tightly round them
And caps pulled down about their ears.

A tumbler full of lukewarm milk
The Englishman provides in haste
And a goblet full of gin
Which Preciosa will not taste.

And while she tells her story weeping
And they are listening, without pause
Against the roof-top tiles above them
The wind in fury gnashed his jaws.

Trans. Roy Campbell

Of all Spanish painters, it is El Greco whose reputation
has undergone the greatest and most startling reassess-
ment. Today no critic could take the patronizing tone
of Théophile Gautier, who saw two of his works in the
hospital of the Cardinal at Toledo in 1840.

POOR EL GRECO

There are also in this church two pictures by Domenico
Theotocopuli, called El Greco, a strange, extravagant painter
who is hardly known outside Spain. His mania, as you know,
was the fear of being taken for an imitator of Titian, whose
pupil he was; this anxiety threw him into the most fantastic
affectations and caprices.

One of these pictures, representing the Holy Family, must
have made poor El Greco very unhappy, for at the first glance
one would take it for a genuine Titian. The ardent tones of the
colour, the brilliant hues of the draperies, that lovely amber-
yellow light which gives warmth even to the coldest tones of the
Venetian painter, all combine to deceive the most practised
eye; only the touch is less broad and liquid. What little reason

121

was left to El Greco must entirely have foundered in the dark seas of madness after finishing this masterpiece; there are not many painters nowadays who are capable of going mad for such a reason.

The other picture, of which the subject is the Baptism of Christ, belongs entirely to El Greco's second manner: an abuse of black and white, violent contrasts, peculiar colours, contorted attitudes, and draperies creased and crumpled in wanton folds; but it is all inspired by a depraved energy, a morbid power which reveal the great painter and the madman of genius. Few pictures have interested me as much as those of El Greco, for the worst of them have always something unexpected, which soars beyond the possible in such a way as to startle you and make you dream.

Un Voyage en Espagne, 1840

Goya's life spanned the Napoleonic Wars. He was forty-five at the time of the French Revolution and died thirteen years after Waterloo. It was a period when world politics must have seemed as upsetting to contemporaries as ours do to us. Of his many paintings in various styles, my own favourites, if that is the right word, are the horrifying fantasies he created on his studio walls, now to be seen at the Prado. They make today's science-fiction cartoons seem homely.

FRANCISCO GOYA

The War of Independence showed to astonished Europe that centuries of despotism, the reign of favourites, and general misgovernment had still left intact the patriotism and strength of the Spanish people. Thus the painter Francisco Goya (1746–1828), at the end of the 18th century, once more introduced to us, through the medium of his painting, that old Spain, the Spain of the great comedy-writers, which fell a prey to the slow but sure process of destruction after the restoration of the Bourbons. Goya, indeed, painted everything, even *Church Pictures* . . . but no man and no period was less naturally adapted for that kind of work. No one will look at his religious pieces until he has first become interested in him on other grounds. In his *Portraits* he has, perhaps, pushed the unvarnished truthfulness of the 17th century to the point of brutality. His *Family of Charles IV* is a satire, which suggests and renders credible the most disreputable chronicles of the secret history of the times. His painting is cold and heavy with black as its dominant tone. But we forget this as we stand before those innumerable improvised figures and scenes in which, with a rare genius for the typical and the momentary, he has for ever imprisoned life, both in its most striking and its most trivial phases, with his brush and burin. Goya's etchings of *Bull Fights*, *Scenes of Madrid Life, The Inquisition*, and the series known as *"Los Caprichos"* form the most valued plates in the portfolio of the collector of Spanish scenes. In his *Dos de Mayo* he has fixed for ever, with demonic power, two terrible moments of the War of Independence; in the blood-curdling *Desastres de la Guerra* he has held the mirror up to war. At the same time no one has so thoroughly understood the irrepressible and intensive gaiety of the Spaniard's enjoyment of life in his festive moments.

PROFESSOR CARL JUSTI, 1908

Velázquez, to me, was a more slowly acquired taste. Pritchett, again, has been the most revealing guide.

DWARFS AND PRINCESSES

At the first acquaintance, with Velásquez's portraits of the court of Philip IV, even with that enchanting picture of the naughty Princess, *Las Meninas*, or with the picture of those arrogant and stubborn dwarfs, one sees the infinitely patient copyist who never conveys more than the visual scene before him; but presently we observe he is a painter of light, a critic of reflections. We see that he has caught the trance of human watchfulness, as if he had caught a few hard grains of time itself. Life is something pinned down by light and time. He has frozen a moment, yet we shall feel that it is a moment at its extreme point; that is, on the point of becoming another moment. If he is the most minute observer in the world, notice how his subjects are caught, themselves also minutely watching the world, with all the concentration the hard human ego is capable of. This is what living is to the human animal; it is to look. To look is to be. We see in Velásquez, as in all the Spaniards, the marriage of mind and eye. No painting could be, in the northern sense, less suggestive of a life without other accoutrement than the body and the habit of the hour.

The sensibility, the pride, the sensuous weakness of the court of Philip IV, where the decadence put out its first flowers in Spanish life, before the fruit formed and rotted, are seen in the realism of Velásquez. In an earlier painter like Zurbarán, in Greco, even in Murillo, and finally in Goya, the same basic psychological dramatic realism can be seen. We cannot doubt

123

that thus life was, was seen and felt to be. And it is part of the genius of such exact penetration to horrify us with the tacit questions: What for? To what end? Behind such certainty is the certainty of death. The mad pride of the Duchess of Alba, her eccentric vanity! The homely foolishness of Charles IV, the total crookedness of Fernando VII!

The Spanish Temper

Song and Dance

Donde hay musica no puede haber cosa mala.
"Where there's music there's no evil."

Spanish saying

It is, of course, of *cante flamenco*, or *cante hondo*, the gypsy music of Andalusia, that one thinks when one thinks of Spanish music. Probably the word "flamenco" referred to the Flemish settlers in Spain, and because they represented all that was odd and fantastic, came to have this meaning. The Andalusians still describe an eccentric person as *muy flamenco*, and the word became attached to the gypsies because they were more fantastic and eccentric than anyone else. Until 1922, when the Spanish composer Falla organized a congress of flamenco-singers at Granada, flamenco was little known and generally looked down on in other parts of Spain. Now it can be heard all over the country. I think it is the most exciting and moving of all folk-music.

FLAMENCO

I first encountered flamenco on a moonlight night in Granada, when, with an American companion, I had just come out of the only cabaret Granada boasted. Let it be said, once and for all, that Spanish cabarets are very bad. I was in a mood of disgust and disgruntlement, and reproached my companion with the waste of one of the few nights left to me in Granada. And, suddenly, there was the sound of a guitar.

Briefly, we were invited by a party of gentlemen who had engaged the *patio* of a neighbouring tavern for a night of flamenco to join their company, and thus I heard my first flamenco singing, and first met Francisco Gálvez Gómez.

Here indeed was the pattern of the great amateur of flamenco and of the Andalucían gentleman: a creature of the sun, inevitably attracting all that is gay, honest, generous and wholesome to his vicinity. Short, broad, fair rather than dark, with the grey Granadino eye alert with humour, Frasquito, as he was generally known, was a popular hero, and knew it; not in the unpleasant sense of personal vanity, but of looking upon it as rather a serious responsibility. . . .

What, it may be asked, are the qualities that make a flamenco singer?

It is not a matter of voice, for at a *concurso de flamenco* that I attended, when Frasquito was a judge, the first place was awarded to a woman whose thin thread of vocal sound was hardly audible beyond the judges' platform, and must have been wholly inaudible from the farther galleries. Like all flamenco singers, she sat to sing; she leaned her forehead on her hand, as though she were weeping.

The necessary technical equipment consists, apparently, in excessive flexibility of the vocal cords, and an almost super-human control of the diaphragm muscle, so that the breath remains boxed in the thoracic cavity as long as it pleases the singer to continue his cadenza—which is a matter dependent entirely on his inspiration and his skill.

But the true art of the flamenco rests in the inspiration itself: in the richness and variety of the improvisation and in its emotional content. There is also the curious, occult liaison which establishes itself between the singer and the past, the singer and his accompanist. To make sure of this liaison, it is common for the singer to rest his hand on the accompanist's knee or shoulder, to lean towards him, or to press his foot against the other's. No signs are exchanged; it is purely a matter of contact, of making a channel for the communication of the singer's intention to the player's mind. Sometimes the channel is unnecessary; the two sit apart, even turned from each other, and some of the singer's postures and movements are curious in the extreme.

It can hardly be sufficiently emphasized that in true flamenco singing there is no element whatever of the theatrical; that therefore all flamenco performances that take place in the theatre lose quality, are falsified and altogether inferior to what one may hear in the *patio*, in the tavern, in the garden or the cave.

The state of flamenco singing is a state of trance; a state of spiritual withdrawal, in which the singer sinks deep within himself, and becomes less and less conscious of his audience. The effect, at the height of the performance, might almost be described as mediumistic: the eyes close, or become set and vacant, an expression of torment distorts the features, which drain themselves of colour, even to the lips. The singer bends, writhes, doubles his body as though suffering an excruciating torture; the sweat glistens on his brow, an arm curves itself strangely, the fingers crisped, as though in the act of tearing something out of the singer's soul. . . .

The songs themselves fall into classes, of which, from the foreigner's point of view, the fandangos and fandangillos are probably the most diverting, with their rough *brio*, to which contributes, not only the guitar but the much louder, more startling bandurría. These songs are very noisy, very gay, and usually serve to "warm up" the atmosphere and to establish the current of good fellowship upon which the success of the evening depends. In particular, they lend themselves to dancing, and, if there is a gipsy present, it is during the fandangillo that she will stride forward, to take up her insolent posture, to loud cries of *"Olé, la gitana!"—"Anda!"—"Guapísima!"*

The jerk of the head, the shaking of shoulders and breasts, the frenzied roll of the hips, snapping of the fingers, rattling of high heels and serpent-like bending of the body are followed with growing excitement by the audience, which contributes to and emphasizes the rhythm with hand clapping. One thing is certain—that however discreetly the dancing may begin, it will by the end of the evening have reached a pitch of lively obscenity, gestures losing their classic formality and becoming more and more broadly specific, and the phallic significance of the dance emerging with the gradual absorption of the spectators into the spirit of the performance. . . .

The test of the flamenco singer comes with the *solea*, whose grave and classic character demands altogether another calibre of interpretation. Soleas are not given, except by request, to foreign audiences, which, it is taken for granted, neither appreciate nor respect their recondite qualities. This was amusingly demonstrated to me when, having arranged for a flamenco evening at a certain price, my host was asked for a hundred pesetas more than the agreed fee. When, naturally, he protested, the naïve explanation was forthcoming, that the singers had only expected to give the usual range of subjects which had proved acceptable to foreigners, but the señora had asked for soleas and martinetes! . . .

The *martinete* is my favourite flamenco form, but I have only once heard it sung well. . . . This song of the chain-gang prisoners, unlike most song-forms, has many verses; it is almost alarming, as the song progresses, to watch its effect on the singer. His eyes sink back in his head, the skin tightens on his face, becomes livid; gradually he slips sidelong in his chair, his hands fall lifeless, the knuckles trailing on the ground; his voice fades.

MARGUERITE STEEN *Granada Window*, 1949

IN A CELLAR IN MADRID

Performances of this kind, in which some players fasten themselves on the tourist and give their performance, are usually paid for with a bottle of brandy and a cigarette or two; or, in smarter surroundings when there is a special invitation, by money. One pays up and hopes for the best, but we had a large, quiet Yorkshireman in our party whose air of Saxon shyness concealed a deep knowledge of the Spanish vernacular and an obstinate respect for correct procedure. Our young gypsy made the error of asking the Yorkshireman a special fee because he was a professional artist giving an unusual performance, and when this was refused there was a characteristic row. It began on the doorstep of the cellar, continued in the street, trailed down to the middle of the Puerta del Sol. It was a hot night; the clock on the Ministry of the Interior coldly struck four, while the gypsy shouted, the Yorkshireman answered back. The gypsy called for a witness. At four in the morning the recognized authority of the streets is the night watchman. They came out one by one from their doorways like the Watch of Fielding's London, and with them the strange night population who sleep out in doorways or the streets. The gypsy stuck out his chest, produced his official papers. The crowd listened. A woman, a lottery-ticket seller, recommended going to the police station, and on the whole the crowd were against us, until the gypsy made the fatal mistake of overplaying his hand. From his papers he picked out some document.

"I am an artist," he cried. They nodded sympathetically.

"I was a soldier of Franco," he added, showing more papers. They stepped back from him at once.

"None of that," someone said politely.

Among the common people of Madrid one is not likely to get very far with being a soldier of Franco.

The dispute now left the chest-baring, chest-thumping, and paper-showing stage, to insults like:

"You are boring me. Go away."

"On the contrary, it is you who are boring me."

The quarrel trailed off to the police station, but within sight of it the gypsy gave in. It was now the time for face-saving. The gypsy said he had no wish to quarrel. The Yorkshireman said he loved the greatness of the Spanish nation. The gypsy said he loved the greatness of the English nation. A year later I was astonished to see my friends had engaged this gypsy to sing again. He had a young wife now. The gypsy was not at all surprised. Such rows are common in Spain.

"It is better," he said, "to begin a friendship with a little aversion."

v. s. PRITCHETT *The Spanish Temper*

In the 1860s Matilda Betham Edwards also fell under the Gypsy influence.

CAPTAIN ANTONIO'S SPELL

After disappointing us on several occasions, Captain Antonio came. He had pleaded a sore finger as excuse for his delay, but I am inclined to think that he waited in expectation of a larger audience and more dollars; for the arrival of an American family healed the Captain's finger miraculously fast. It was sore in the morning, very bad indeed! and, lo and behold! in the evening it was quite well; but let that pass—Captain Antonio's music made us very forgiving.

He came in—a tall, superbly built man in the prime of life, with a tawny skin, eyes of extraordinary brilliancy, receding jaws, and very low brow, long narrow throat, and altogether, of an Egyptian, ancient look, as if he had been one of the old Nile gods come to life.

He bowed graciously, threw off his Spanish cloak, for the gitanos, like all the rest of the world, are growing conventional now, losing costume and characteristics every day; and commenced tuning his guitar.

It was a wretchedly poor instrument, and we began to wonder what sort of torments were about to be inflicted on us, when, on a sudden, the tuning ceased and the music seized hold of us like galvanism. For it was such music as one had never dreamed of before. His fingers but touch the chords, and all at once your breath is taken away, your blood is warmed as if by strong wine, your brain whirls, your eyes see visions, your ears hear marvellous voices, your senses are all mastered by a power that seems to shake the very spheres.

You see the strangest forms and faces, imp, devil, witch, and wizard; you hear a jargon of voices, in love, in anger, in war, in worship, in joy, in despair. Beautiful gitanos come in the charmed circle, join hands, dance for a moment and vanish, or it is filled by a gipsy camp—the fires are blazing, you see men and women feasting, singing, making love, when, all at once, a cry of alarm is heard, and the scene is changed to bloodshed and horrors. Every phase of savage life is brought before your eyes and made real, as if you were tasting it in the flesh. You are indeed for the nonce a gipsy, and know what the gipsy's world is, above, below, in heaven and in hell; your pulses are quickened to gipsy pitch, you are ready to make love and war, to heal and slay, to wander to the world's end, to be outlawed and hunted down, to dare to do anything for the sake of the sweet, untrammelled life of the tent, the bright blue sky, the mountain air, the free savagedom, the joyous dance, the passionate friendship, the fiery love.

Through Spain to the Sahara

To an eighteenth-century Englishman the Fandango clearly resembled the Twist, and was about as shocking.

THE FANDANGO

Our evening ended with a ball, where we had for the first time the pleasure of seeing the Fandango danced. It is odd and entertaining enough, when they execute with perfection and agility all the various footings, wheelings of the arms, and crackings of the fingers; but it exceeds in wantonness all the dances I ever beheld. Such motions, such writhings of the body and positions of the limbs, as no modest eye can look upon without a blush! A good Fandango lady will stand five minutes in one spot, wriggling like a worm that has just been cut in two.

THE GUITAR

All these nights past we have heard the people singing doleful ditties under our windows to the sound of a guitar, which they strike with their nails, without any notion of air, but merely as a kind of an accompaniment, sometimes high, sometimes low, but very coarse and monotonous. I can compare their music to nothing so well as to the beating of a frying-pan, to call down a swarm of bees.

HENRY SWINBURNE *Travels through Spain*, 1779

TARANTELLA

Do you remember an Inn,
Miranda?
Do you remember an Inn?
And the tedding and the spreading
Of the straw for a bedding,
And the fleas that tease in the High Pyrenees,
And the wine that tasted of the tar?
And the cheers and the jeers of the young muleteers
(Under the vine of the dark verandah)?
Do you remember an Inn, Miranda,
Do you remember an Inn?
And the cheers and the jeers of the young muleteers
Who hadn't got a penny,
And who weren't paying any,

And the hammer at the doors and the Din?
And the Hip! Hop! Hap!
Of the clap
Of the hands to the twirl and the swirl
Of the girl gone chancing,
Glancing,
Dancing,
Backing and advancing,
Snapping of a clapper to the spin
Out and in—
And the Ting, Tong, Tang of the Guitar!
Do you remember an Inn,
Miranda?
Do you remember an Inn?

Never more;
Miranda,
Never more.
Only the high peaks hoar:
And Aragon a torrent at the door.
No sound
In the walls of the Halls where falls
The tread
Of the feet of the dead to the ground
No sound:
But the boom
Of the Waterfall like Doom.

HILAIRE BELLOC *Sonnets and Verse*, 1923

Though flamenco is now universal, every part of Spain
has its own traditional songs and dances. Elliot Paul
lived on the small Balearic island of Ibiza till the Civil
War came.

BEFORE THE WAR

In the happy days of Santa Eulalia, the moon shone over the
land without the chill in the air that elsewhere makes the night
inhospitable, and from May until November the men sat long
hours after dinner in front of the cafés, drinking anis, cognac,
cazalla or beer or the strong red wine of the country. They
talked, argued, sang songs from Valencia or Aragon or native to
Ibiza, ranging in mood from nostalgia to ribaldry. I can hear
now, as I write (and I wish I could not), their voices in a
favourite refrain.

Petiquita meua	"My little cigarette box,
Que buida qu'estas	How empty you are!
Que buida qu'estas	How empty you are!
Pero demá es Diumenge	But to-morrow is Sunday
Yo tu rempliras	And I'll fill you.
Yo tu rempliras	And I'll fill you."

Chorus
Dos cigarros ting	"I have two cigarettes.
Tres quil vol fumar	Three (friends) want to smoke.
Dos y tres fon cinq	Two and three make five,
Y cinq fon dao	And five make ten,
Y dao fon vint.	And ten make twenty.

Vint menus cinq fon quinze	Twenty minus five make fifteen.
Quinze menus cinq fon dao	Fifteen minus five make ten.
Dao menus cinq fon cinq	Ten minus five make five,
Y cinq fon dao	And five make ten,
Y dao fon vint.	And ten make twenty."

There is much in that song evocative of the character of Santa Eulalia and of Spain, the wistful attitude towards that which has contributed to pleasure, the acknowledgment of temporary material insufficiency with hope expressed immediately afterwards, a joy in speculative patterns which expand and contract so effortlessly. The same feelings, translated into terms of national finance, defence or self-government, have chaotic results. They make for agreeable citizens but not zealous ones, brave soldiers who are born to lose a fight bravely.

The Life and Death of a Spanish Town, 1937

Captain Carleton heard the music of Valencia in the year 1708 on this sad occasion.

EXCEPT IN VALENCIA

I just now distinguished, by an exception, the music of Valencia, where alone I experienced the use of the violin; which, though I cannot, in respect to other countries, call good, yet, in respect to the other parts of Spain, I must acknowledge it much the best. . . .

I will speak of the best I heard, which was on this unfortunate occasion: several natives of that country, having received sentence of death for their adherence to King Charles, were accordingly ordered to the place of execution. It is the custom there, on all such occasions, for all the music of the city to meet near the gallows, and play the most affecting and melancholy airs, to the very approach of the condemned; and really the music was so moving, it heightened the scene of sorrow, and brought compassion into the eyes even of enemies.

As to the condemned, they came stript of their own clothes, and covered with black frocks, in which they were led along the streets to the place of execution, the friars praying all the way. When they came through any street, where any public images were fixed, they staid before them some reasonable time in prayer with the friars. When they arrived at the fatal place, those fathers leave them not, but continue praying and giving them ghostly encouragement, standing upon the rounds of the ladder till they are turned off. The hangman always wears a silver badge of a ladder to distinguish his profession: but his manner of executing his office had somewhat in it too singular to allow of silence. When he had tied fast the hands of the criminal, he rested his knee upon them, and with one hand on the criminal's nostrils, to stop his breath the sooner, threw himself off the ladder along with the dying party. This he does to expedite his fate; though, considering the force, I wonder it does not tear head and body asunder; which yet I never heard that it did.

CAPTAIN GEORGE CARLETON *Memoirs*

As in most other ways, the Basques are different.

AURRESKU AND SWORD DANCE

The *aurresku* is surely far more than a mere dance—it is the national symbol of the Basque race. As I watched the solemn expressions of the youths as they danced in front of the girls, I was conscious that this dance was part of the ritual of Basque life. The reception of the young couples by the Mayor of the town, the procession into the square, the dance itself, were all parts of a national dramatic spectacle. In this spectacle the men play a preponderant rôle. The leader is called the *aurresky*, or "first hand", and he sends four men to fetch his *novia*. After he has performed in front of her he leads her into the dance. He and the *atzesku*, or last hand, who is at the end of the line, direct the various complicated figures. As each lady is invited to dance by her cavalier a special leitmotif is played.

The whole dance seems to have been expressly created to show off the strength and grace of the triumphant hero who is wooing his fair lady. He makes incredible jumps and performs acrobatic feats in opposition to any rival who may want to become her suitor and finally carries her off as his prize. The lady's part is to watch discreetly and bestow favours. I noticed too that the young man when dancing with his *novia* did not clasp her by the hand, but held one end of a white silk hander-chief while she held the other—a delicate proof of the modesty of Basques.

After we had seen the *aurresku* we saw the "Sword-Dance" which is characteristic of the province of Guipúzcoa. I had expected to witness a performance similar to the brawny Scottish sword-dance where the weapons are crossed upon the ground and a kilted warrior dances fiercely between the blades. The Basque sword-dance is more of a pageant than a dance. The young men were dressed in white shirt and trousers with red *boina* and sash. When the band played a march tune they all formed up four abreast and the leader danced solo in front of them kicking his legs high up in the air. The music, which was slow and heavily accented in 5/8 time, gradually increased in tempo as the rest of the dancers followed the example of the leader. Each of them had a sword in his hand covered with a handkerchief and as the lines closed in and opened out, the swords crossed in battle. I have never seen a more martial dance or one more calculated to excite men to battle: the music blared, the drums beat the inexorable rhythm, the sword-blades shone in the sun, the people in the square shouted with enthusiasm. One of the dancers suddenly fell to the ground amidst the forest of gleaming blades and straightway he was raised up by his companions as though he was a chief who had been killed in battle. Since it was originally a warrior's dance, it is customary to divide the dancers into two camps—one called the Christians—the other the Moors.

WALTER STARKIE *Spanish Raggle-Taggle*, 1934

When I was taught, and I must admit enjoyed, English Morris dancing at school by an enthusiastic master who dressed us in ribbons and bells, he never told us it had a Spanish origin. Perhaps he didn't know.

MORRIS—OR MOORISH

Dancing at all is a novelty among Spanish ladies, which was introduced with the Bourbons. As among the Romans and Moors, it was before thought undignified. Performers were hired to amuse the inmates of the Christian harem; to mix and change hands with men was not to be thought of for an instant; and to this day few Spanish women shake hands with men—the shock is too electrical; they only give them with their hearts, and for good.

The lower classes, who are a trifle less particular, and among whom, by the blessing of Santiago, the foreign dancing-master is not abroad, adhere to the primitive steps and tunes of their Oriental forefathers. Their accompaniments are the "tabret and the harp", the guitar, the tambourine, and the castanet. The essence of these instruments is to give a noise on being beaten. Simple as it may seem to play on the latter, it is only attained by a quick ear and finger, and great practice; accordingly these delights of the people are always in their hands . . . they take to it before their alphabet, since the very urchins in the street begin to learn by snapping their fingers, or clicking together two shells or bits of slate, to which they dance. . . . All night long, three thousand years ago, say the historians, did they dance and sing, or rather jump and *yell*, to these "*howl*ings of Tarshish"; and so far from its being a fatigue, they kept up the ball all night, by way of *resting*.

The Gallicians and Asturians retain among many of their aboriginal dances and tunes, a wild Pyrrhic jumping, which, with their shillelah in hand, is like the Gaelic Ghillee Callum, and is the precise Iberian armed dance which Hannibal had performed at the impressive funeral of Gracchus. These quadrille figures are intricate and warlike, requiring, as was said of the Iberian performances, much leg-activity, for which the wiry sinewy active Spaniards are still remarkable. These are the Morris dances imported from Gallicia by our John of Gaunt, who supposed they were Moorish. The peasants still dance them in their best costumes, to the antique castanet, pipe, and tambourine. They are usually directed by a master of ceremonies, or what is equivalent, a parti-coloured fool.

RICHARD FORD *Gatherings from Spain*

Also in Galicia Anthony Carson had trouble with a local folk instrument.

THE DUEL

I hadn't been long in Santiago before I met a man called Jonathan Speed. He was a plump man with far-away belligerent eyes who had come to Galicia to study cathedrals. But it was obvious that he was in search of something else, a private phantom, a strange unedited solution.

One day we heard some bagpipes. They were as wild as wind in the heather, stark with the naked cries of happy murderers in the glens, as Scotch as Haggis, or as Irish as promises. "Astounding," said Speed, "to hell with cathedrals and progressive jazz. Let us buy bagpipes."

Somebody told us about a master bagpipe manufacturer called Pablo. He made the bagpipes in front of your very eyes as another man makes hats or cigars. And when he had fluted the bagpipes he put the pipe to his lips and Pan blazed in the shop. Pan, and no other. Wonderful, insuperable, lost Pan. "The very thing," said Speed, and we went to the shop with one of those eternal Spanish friends who hunt for you everything from sardines to saints. There, in a lost street, crumpled with children, we entered a shop sweet with new sharpened wood, the hum of a lathe, and the royal red blaze of the bagpipe blowers.

"Make me a bagpipe," said Speed.

"And make me a bagpipe without the bag," I said.

In half an hour the bagpipes were on the counter and in another quarter of an hour I had a pipe as gay as a tinker's donkey. Speed slung the bag over his shoulder, blew on the pipe, there was a roar like a stuck pig, and a tune came out as brave as a field in May. It was a Northumbrian air, but it made no difference. I blew on my pipe and there was nothing but wind. "Dance," said Speed, so I danced a vague Hiberian dance, and the children scuttled into the shop and Pablo himself raised the fluted pipe to his mouth and the sawdust room was a world of glow-worms. Later we went from feast to feast until one day he suddenly put on a black suit and a homburg hat and left for England. "My work," he said. Poetry or progressive jazz or cathedrals? I didn't ask him. I am English, but I don't understand the English.

I was alone with the pipe. I started to blow it in my small hotel high up above the Civil Guards, the commercial travellers, the pigs and the hens and the bells. I blew and I blew and not a note came out, just a sound like wind in the wainscoting, like old men coughing over their pipes in a ruined dormitory. I packed my bags, paid my bill and left for the village of Ribeira at the end of a bay and went up into the hills. "Look out for wolves, eagles and ghosts," said an old female domestic who occasionally threw a bucket of water into the Stone Age latrine. She told me about an eagle which had killed an elderly councillor in the town hall. "It sat outside the window and stared at him," she said. "He died of fright." They came from Portugal and might be dead relatives.

Up in the hills were wonderful wild flowers and tiny bees so industrious that they made you ashamed. I blew on the pipe and certain notes rang on the air like drowned bells. There are seven apertures on the pipe, unevenly placed, and the fingers have to be as nimble as spiders. Also the breath must flow like a great slow bellows, and the head hold a discipline of harmony, born and slowly learnt. The first pattern of music was a small broken Moorish melody, it got itself caught in the pipe on its way from Marrakesh or the tinkling markets of Tiznit. I played this tune over and over again and got stung by a bee. This was

A MAN AND HIS DONKEY

A good-sized one this, so that he can stretch his toes. But it would be no disgrace if his heels did touch the ground. A donkey's a donkey and a lot better than no donkey

FIGHTING COCKS

Another view of our own mediaeval past. Not a pretty one, perhaps, but with admirable indifference the Spanish still do it. Is it now legal? Probably, but no one seems certain

not what I sought. I craved the lilt of the early Galician days, when Irish giants sat on their thrones and the story-tellers sat under the cedars. And at last, among the wild lilies and the heather, a minute gasping melody flowed from the pipe. I do not know how. I don't necessarily believe in inspiration and wouldn't care to state that there are obvious reasons for everything. We all have the secret ground which is ourselves—it runs counter to so many orthodox arguments. For me, writing is a certain craft which matures through repetition, but some times, in painting, about which I know nothing, I can capture the whole of a small world in a few seconds.

I repeated this pattern of notes, and lay back on the heather. A seagull floated over my head but did not speak. About ten minutes later I heard a flurry over the grass, a rustling, and a patter of horn and hoof, and looked around. I was surrounded by sheep. Roughly there must have been about five hundred, which meant a thousand eyes, perplexed, inquiring and cold with the cold doubt of sheep. They stood there, ciphers of wool and mutton, with a blaze in their brains. I have never heard of a man being attacked by sheep, but who could tell? I remembered about the eagles and ghosts and stood up. Far away I could hear a man shouting, and presently saw him, a black figure with a looming face. He was waving a pipe, the same fluted shape as mine, and suddenly he sat down, put it to his lips and blew. There was tremble in the wind, a spell of silver and sunlight, and the sheep teetered on their hooves, flickered their eyes and disappeared. I sat down and looked at the pipe. I held a fascinating power. It was impossible to resist it. I put it to my lips and blew and the notes scampered over the heather like hares on a bright morning. I hadn't long to wait. In another minute the sheep were back, ringing me round with a wild, thin, staring hope. I was the new Messiah of a grassy Salvation. Again I could hear the man shouting, and I got up and walked back to the village, and entered the inn and began drinking at the bar.

"A good day?" asked the proprietor, polishing the glasses.

"A good day," I said. "I've learnt to play a tune on the bagpipe."

"Play it," said the proprietor with a laugh.

I lifted the pipe to my lips and the notes fell out of it like dice.

" I never heard a tune like that," said the proprietor, filling my glass.

It was about five minutes later that the first sheep trotted into the inn.

Looking for a Bandit

137

The Bullfight

El sol es el mejor torero.
"The sun is the best bullfighter."

Spanish saying

I think it is the most cultured festival that exists anywhere in the world. It is the only place where one can go in safety to contemplate Death surrounded by the most dazzling beauty. What would happen to the Spanish springtime, to Spanish blood, and even to the Spanish language if the trumpets of the bullring should ever cease to sound?

F. G. LORCA

Not everyone would agree with Lorca. Many Spaniards see bullfighting as a hangover from a barbaric past which they should be ashamed of and quickly abolish. I find it wildly exciting. Without being an *aficionado*, I like the drama and shock and the knowledge that this is something more real than an entertainment, even if I am not quite sure what it is. But without expert knowledge, and without the Spanish appetite for repetition, I do not want to see the same drama more than once or perhaps twice in an afternoon.

Whether one is for or against it, bullfighting seems to the foreigner not only peculiarly Spanish, but a public demonstration of many inescapable Spanish character-istics—not least of them this one.

A SPANISH PROPENSITY

Baiting a bull in any shape is irresistible to the lower orders of Spain, who disregard injuries to the bodies, and, what is worse, to their cloaks. The hostility to the horned beast is instinctive, and grows with their growth, until it becomes . . . a second nature. The young urchins in the streets play at *"toro"*, as ours do at leap-frog; they go through the whole mimic spectacle amongst each other, observing every law and rule, as our schoolboys do when they fight. Few adult Spaniards, when journeying through the country, ever pass a herd of cows without this dormant propensity breaking out; they provoke the animals to fight by waving their cloaks or *capas*, a challenge hence called *el capeo*.

RICHARD FORD Gatherings from Spain

Where bullfighting originated isn't certain. Some say Crete, and there is the legend of Theseus and the Minotaur, but when I recently saw the most famous bull fresco found in the Cretan palace at Knossos I agreed with those who say this may show bull acrobatics but not bullfighting. Whatever its origins, it came to Spain with the Moors and was adopted by Christian Spain as a sport for the aristocracy, a form of practice for battle or tournament. In this, its early form, a knight alone fought the bull from a horse with lance or short spear.

Horseback bullfighting can still be seen in Spain today. The first bullfight I ever saw, at Palma, was in the Portuguese style in which most of the early playing of the bull is done from a horse, but adapted for Spanish tastes so that the torero dismounted to kill. He seemed hopelessly inexpert on his feet and was twice knocked down before he managed it. In Richard Ford's time the old-style horseback bull fighting was reserved for special days and impoverished knights.

ROYAL BULLFIGHTS

They are only given at Madrid, and then are conducted entirely after the ancient Spanish and Moorish customs. . . . They take place in the great square of the capital, which is then converted into an arena. The windows of the quaint and lofty houses are arranged as boxes, and hung with velvets and silks. The royal family is seated under a canopy of state in the balcony of the central mansion. . . . On these royal occasions the bulls are assailed by gentlemen, dressed and armed as in good old Spanish times, before the fatal Bourbon accession obliterated Castilian costume, customs and nationality. The champions, clad in the fashions of the Philips, and mounted on beauteous barbs, the minions of their race, attack the fierce animal with only a short spear, the immemorial weapon of the Iberian. The combatants must be hidalgos by birth, and have each a *padrino*, or god-father, a first grandee of Spain, who passes before royalty in a splendid equipage and six, and is attended by bands of running footmen, who are arrayed either as Greeks, Romans, Moors, or fancy characters. It is not easy to obtain these *caballeros en plaza*, or poor knights, who are willing to expose their lives to the imminent dangers, albeit during the fight they have the benefit of experienced *toreros* to advise their actions and cover their retreats.

In 1833 a gentle dame, without the privity of her lord and husband, inscribed his name as one of the champion volunteers. In procuring him this agreeable surprise, she, so it was said in Madrid, argued thus: "Either *mi marido* will be killed—in that case I shall get a new husband; or he will survive, in which event he will get a pension." She failed in both of these admirable calculations—such is the uncertainty of human events. The terror of this poor *héros malgré lui*, on whom chivalry had been thrust, was absolutely ludicrous when exposed by his well-intentioned better-half, to the horns of this dilemma and bull. Any other horns, my dearest, but these! He was wounded at the first rush, did survive, and did not get a pension; for Ferdinand died soon after, and few pensions have been paid in the Peninsula, since the land has been blessed with a *charte*, constitution, liberty, and a representative government.

Gatherings from Spain

Till only a few years ago the audience of a bullfight, if the bull was cowardly, could call for *fuego*—explosive *banderillas*, or *perros*—the dogs.

THE DOGS

In vain the picadors spurred him and the *banderilleros* drove in their *banderilles*, nothing would induce him to fight, and the crowd began to shout for the *perros*, that is, the dogs.

The alguazil directed an enquiring glance at the Queen's box, received permission and gave his orders. Immediately everyone in the arena drew away from the bull as though the poor animal had the plague, and he stood alone in the midst of the arena, perhaps thinking that now he was left in peace he would be led back to the quiet mountains where he was reared. If so his dream was in vain. The gate opened. One after another there entered six men each carrying a hound that furiously gave tongue at sight of the bull. On seeing them the bull guessed what was to happen and backed up against the barrier. In a second the baying pack had crossed the arena and the battle began. Against these new antagonists, his natural enemies, the bull recovered his spirits and showed more courage. As for the dogs, they were well-bred mastiffs and bull-dogs, the smallest and fiercest of all being a bull-dog from London. One dog was thrown into the midst of the crowd. Another, tossed straight up into the air, fell on the barrier and broke its back. The others, trampled underfoot, managed to get up again and two of them seized the bull's ears, another, the smallest one, gripped his muzzle and the forth made him turn. Overcome with pain the bull gave a fearful bellow and tried to flee from this ever-growing agony, but the dogs held firm. Twice he encircled the arena, dashed to right and left, shook himself, rolled in the sand and bucked like a horse. All was useless. The jaws that held him stayed firmly locked and at last he stood defeated, his head down, while the dogs dragged him to his knees. A bull that has to be baited by hounds is considered unworthy of the matador's sword and of the stroke from the front, between the shoulders, so one of the *chulos* came forward and thrust his sword into the great beast's flank. His third blow reached the heart and the bull fell prone.

ALEXANDRE DUMAS *From Paris to Cadiz*

Hemingway, best known of all hispanophiles, set his novel *The Sun Also Rises* largely at the famous San Fermín fiesta at Pamplona. It is my favourite Hemingway, perhaps my favourite novel. Besides this and his Spanish Civil War novel, *For Whom the Bell Tolls*, he has written what remains the most authoritative and persuasive defence in English of bullfighting: *Death in the Afternoon*.

THE HORSE

The question of why the death of the horse in the bull ring is not moving, not moving to some people that is, is complicated; but the fundamental reason may be that the death of the horse tends to be comic while that of the bull is tragic. In the tragedy of the bullfight the horse is the comic character. This may be shocking, but it is true. Therefore the worse the horses are, provided they are high enough off the ground and solid enough so that the picador can perform his mission with the spiked pole, or vara, the more they are a comic element. You should be horrified and disgusted at these parodies of horses and what happens to them, but there is no way to be sure that you will be unless you make up your mind to be, no matter what your feelings. They are so unlike horses; in some ways they are like birds, any of the awkward birds such as the adjutants or the wide-billed storks, and when, lifted by the thrust of the bull's neck and shoulder muscles their legs hang, big hoofs dangling, neck drooping, the worn-out body lifted on the horn, they are not comic; but I swear they are not tragic. The tragedy is all centred in the bull and in the man. The tragic climax of the horse's career has occurred off stage at an earlier time; when he was bought by the horse contractor for use in the bull ring. The end in the ring, somehow, seems not unfitting to the structure of the animal and when the canvases are stretched over the horses, the long legs, and necks, the strange-shaped heads and the canvas covering the body to make a sort of wing, they are more like birds than ever. They look a little as a dead pelican does. A live pelican is an interesting, amusing, and sympathetic bird, though if you handle him he will give you lice; but a dead pelican looks very silly.

This is not being written as an apology for bullfights, but to try to present the bullfight integrally, and to do this a number of things must be admitted which an apologist, making a case, would slide over or avoid. The comic that happens to these horses is not their death then; death is not comic, and gives a temporary dignity to the most comic characters, although this dignity passes once death has occurred; but the strange and burlesque visceral accidents which occur. There is certainly nothing comic by our standards in seeing an animal emptied of its visceral content, but if this animal instead of doing something tragic, gallops in a stiff old-maidish fashion around a ring trailing the opposite of clouds of glory, it is as comic when what it is trailing is real as when the Fratellinis give a burlesque of it in which the viscera are represented by rolls of bandages, sausages and other things. If the one is comic the other is; the humour comes from the same principle. I have seen it, people running, horse emptying, one dignity after another being destroyed in the spattering, and trailing of its innermost values, in a complete burlesque of tragedy. I have seen these, call them disembowellings, that is the worst word, when, due to their timing, they were very funny. This is the sort of thing you should not admit, but it is because such things have not been admitted that the bullfight has never been explained.

These visceral accidents, as I write this, are no longer a part of the Spanish bullfight, as under the government of Primo de Rivera it was decided to protect the abdomens of the horses with a sort of quilted mattress designed in the terms of the decree "to avoid those horrible sights which so disgust foreigners and tourists". These protectors avoid these sights and greatly decrease the number of horses killed in the bull ring, but they in no way decrease the pain suffered by the horses; they take away much of the bravery from the bull . . . and they are the first step towards the suppression of the bullfight. The bullfight is a Spanish institution; it has not existed because of the foreigners and tourists, but always in spite of them, and any step to modify it to secure their approval, which it will never have, is a step towards its complete suppression. . . .

I believe that the tragedy of the bullfight is so well ordered and so strongly disciplined by ritual that a person feeling the whole tragedy cannot separate the minor comic-tragedy of the horse so as to feel it emotionally. If they sense the meaning and end of the whole thing even when they know nothing about it; feel that this thing they do not understand is going on, the business of the horses is nothing more than an incident. If they get no feeling of the whole tragedy naturally they will react emotionally to the most picturesque incident.

If Hemingway is, to my mind, less than convincing about the horses (which incidentally have their vocal chords cut so that they shall not make an offensive noise), he does at his best convince me that bullfighting is an art, not a sport.

ROMERO'S BULL-FIGHT

Romero was the whole show. I do not think Brett saw any other bull-fighter. No one else did either, except the hard-shelled technicians. It was all Romero. There were two other matadors, but they did not count. I sat beside Brett and explained to Brett what it was all about. I told her about watching the bull, not the horse, when the bulls charged the picadors, and got her watching the picador place the point of his pic so that she saw what it was all about, so that it became more something that was going on with a definite end, and less of a spectacle with unexplained horrors. I had her watch how Romero took the bull away from a fallen horse with his cape, and how he held him with the cape and turned him, smoothly and suavely, never wasting the bull. She saw how Romero avoided every brusque movement and saved his bulls for the last when he wanted them, not winded and discomposed but smoothly worn down. She saw how close Romero always worked to the bull, and I pointed out to her the tricks the other bull-fighters used to make it look as though they were working closely. She saw why she liked Romero's cape-work and why she did not like the others.

Romero never made any contortions, always it was straight and pure and natural in line. The others twisted themselves like corkscrews, their elbows raised, and leaned against the flanks of the bull after his horns had passed, to give a faked

143

look of danger. Afterwards, all that was faked turned bad and gave an unpleasant feeling. Romero's bull-fighting gave real emotion, because he kept the absolute purity of line in his movements and always quietly and calmly let the horns pass him close each time. He did not have to emphasize their closeness. Brett saw how something that was beautiful done close to the bull was ridiculous if it were done a little way off.

The Sun Also Rises

Like most English visitors, Nelson went to a bullfight— and misunderstood it.

NELSON'S BULLFIGHT

A bull-feast was exhibited, for which the Spaniards are famous; and from their dexterity in attacking and killing of these animals, the ladies choose their husbands. We English had certainly to regret the want of humanity in the Dons and Donnas. The amphitheatre will hold 16,000 people; about 12,000 were present. Ten bulls were selected, and one brought out at a time. Three cavaliers on horseback, and footmen with flags, were the combatants. We had what is called a fine feast, for five horses were killed, and two men very much hurt: had they been killed, it would have been quite complete. We felt for the bulls and horses; and I own it would not have displeased me to have had some of the Dons tossed by the enraged animal. How women can even sit out, much more applaud, such sights, is astonishing. It even turned us sick, and we could hardly go through it: the dead mangled horses with the entrails torn out, and the bulls covered with blood, were too much. However, we have seen one bull-feast, and agree that nothing shall tempt us to see another. The better sort of people never miss one, if within reach of them; and the lowest will sell his jacket, or go without his victuals, rather than be absent.

Letter to Mrs Nelson, 1793

Bullfighting is, above all, an Andalusian passion. And the bullring at Ronda, in southern Andalusia, is the oldest in Spain. This bullfighting description from one of Lorca's plays is less well known than his Lament for Ignacio Sánchez Mejías, with its recurring refrain "A las cinco de la tarde". In translation, at least, I like it as well.

RONDA BULLRING

In the greatest bullfight ever
At Ronda's ancient circus seen—
Five jet-black bulls, for their devices
Wearing rosettes of black and green . . .
The girls turned up with shrilling voices
In painted gigs and jaunting-cars
Displaying their round fans embroidered
With sequins glittering like stars . . .
The lads of Ronda came in riding
Affected, supercilious mares,
With wide grey hats upon their eyebrows
Pulled slantwise down with rakish airs.
The tiers (all hats and towering combs)
Where people had begun to pack,
Round, like the zodiac, revolving,
Were pied with laughter white and black;
And when the mighty Cayetano
Strode over the straw-coloured sands
Dressed in his apple-coloured costume
Broidered with silk and silver bands,
From all the fighters in the ring
He stood so boldly out alone
Before the great black bulls of jet
Which Spain from her own earth had grown—
The afternoon went gipsy-coloured
Bronzing its tan to match his own.
If you had seen with what a grace
He moved his legs, and seemed to swim;
What equilibrium was his
With cape and swordcloth deft and trim;
Romero torrying the stars
In heaven, could scarcely match with him!
He killed five bulls, five jet-black bulls
Wearing rosettes of black and green.
Upon the sharp point of his sword
Five flowers he opened to be seen.
Grazing the muzzles of the brutes,
Each instant you could see him glide,
Like a great butterfly of gold
With rosy wings fanned open wide.
The circus, with the afternoon
Vibrated, in the uproar swaying;
And in between the scent of blood
That of the mountain-tops went straying.

Marianna Pineda, trans. Roy Campbell

Of all the great Spanish bullfighters it is Juan Belmonte who did most to bring the bullfight as an art to perfection. A child of a poor Spanish family of ten, he was a small, unimpressive man and often ill. He developed his bullfighting technique, in Leslie Charteris' view, partly because of his fantastic courage and partly because he simply hadn't the strength to be continually running from the bull. I find his autobiography the most fascinating of all bullfighting books. As a child this is how he learnt.

THE BROTHERHOOD OF SAN JACINTO

These lads had a new way of practising bullfighting. The customary thing for an *aficionado* to do was to go to *capeas* or get permission from the ranchers to try a pass or two at the trials, where their nervousness and inexperience provided plenty of entertainment for the assembled guests. To the brotherhood of San Jacinto this procedure seemed much too undignified. They went into the country to fight the rancher's bulls without his permission, in defiance of the guards, the constabulary, and the whole majesty of the Law. . . .

It was my job to set out in the afternoon for the Tablada grazing lands to find out if there was any herd about which could be fought. It was a seven- to eight-mile hike across country, and one had to avoid meeting the guards, who had a well-founded distrust of all boys who came near the herd. Then I had to come back and give my friends an account of my explorations, and if there were indeed bulls in the enclosures the expedition was promptly organised. We met at our refreshment stand and fixed the time of our departure so that the moon would be well up when we reached the pastures. We had to take the footpaths to avoid encountering any of the Guardia Civil, and we had to do without a proper cloak because that would have been evidence against us if we were stopped. We used a coat belonging to Riverito, whom we all acknowledged as the most proficient.

When we got to the corral we would separate a promising-looking bull—usually the biggest one we could find. For the most part they were inferior stock, bred for meat rather than fighting; and when we had laboriously separated the animal it would rarely charge without a lot of provocation or until after it had turned round a few times and decided that there was no other way of escape.

Riverito played it first, which was his privilege as the leader. The others patiently waited for their turn, and no one ever dared to butt in before his allotted time. When Riverito had finished, he would pass the coat to the next man, and so we would follow each other in strict order. The social grades of that band of anarchists were religiously respected. The best fighter took the coat first; the least expert was relegated inexorably to the last place. Everyone's position was tacitly recognised by the others, and there was never any other ranking among us than that of unanimously respected merit.

I started by being the last in order, and when all the others had had enough they handed the coat to me to do the best I could with it. Naturally this wasn't much.

But one night something happened that upset all the accepted rules of precedence. Following our custom of playing the largest animal we could find, we had separated a huge bull which attacked from the first moment instead of trying to get away like the others. Accustomed as we were to half-blooded stock which only charged when it was cornered, we were completely disconcerted by the vigorous attack of that mountainous bull which only had to see the shadow of a bullfighter to launch itself at him like a streak of lightning. In four or five rushes it put the fear of God into our party, and very soon it stood alone in the centre of the enclosure with its head in the clouds and its horns goring at the moon, while the gladiators flattened themselves against the fence and urged each other to attract its attention in any direction except their own. But the truth was that nobody wanted to take it on, and the bull was the unquestioned master of the arena.

"Has this bull got us licked?" I thought. "Are we supposed to be fighting it or is it fighting us?"

I waited trembling for a few seconds—I don't know whether with fear or jubilation. It wasn't my turn to take the field, but none of my companions would make a move and the bull was still waiting there. A few paces away lay the coat we were using, which had been lost in the débâcle. I stretched out my arm. When I had the coat in my hand I straightened up and moved slowly towards the bull. It pawed the ground and watched me approach, measuring the distance, and at the exact moment it hurled itself at me like a hurricane. I stood firm and led it past me with the coat. It turned quickly, kicking up a cloud of dust, and again I made it pass me. I had hardly recovered my position when it was on me again. I felt its quivering mass brushing against my body. Again and again I led it past, until at last I gave it a *recorte* which left it rooted to the ground and staring at me as if it couldn't make out what had happened to it. I turned my back on it and carelessly threw down the coat for anyone else to play with who felt like it, and the ovation I was giving myself almost deafened me.

147

After that night I was never again the last to fight. When the leader of the band gave up the coat, I would step forward and take it over as if I was exercising an indisputable right. I had won the position in fair combat, and nobody questioned my superiority. Nevertheless, the truth is that I was never the absolute leader.

Belmonte's experiences as a young torero were sometimes less comforting. He tells a terrifying story of his first corrida at Seville when, exhausted by a new mistress, he was continually knocked down by a cowardly bull and hoped each time that he could at last be carried away only to discover that he wasn't hurt and had to get up and chase it again. He ended on his knees in front of its horns, begging it to kill him, but it had become too bored to charge. At Guareña he had other troubles.

A CONTRACT AT GUAREÑA

When we got to Guareña and saw the bulls, everything that we had been told about them paled before the reality. They were four mammoths of nearly fourteen hundred pounds each, and on top of that three were blind in one eye. There were only two or three miserable little horses to punish them with; and Calderón, on this and other pretexts which his experienced wiliness suggested to him, threatened that we should refuse to fight at all unless they made us certain definite concessions. What he was really aiming at was to get them to pay us some money in advance, because otherwise it was highly problematical whether we should ever collect it. . . .

The time for the corrida drew near, and in view of our attitude the municipal authorities intervened. They put the impresario on one side; and the mayor, the judge, and various other important people tried to talk Calderón round. A long-winded and laborious conference got under way. Meanwhile the populace, not knowing whether the corrida was going to take place or not, was milling rowdily around the bullring. Calderón went in and out of our room with orders and counter-orders.

"Get yourselves dressed. We're going to the ring."

In five minutes he would come back.

"Take your clothes off. We're not going to fight."

I got tired of this suspense, left my costume on a chair, and went for a walk through the town. The infuriated public was on the point of starting a riot. Half an hour after the corrida

148

was supposed to have started, I saw poor old Calderón coming in search of me with three *guardias civiles* round him.

"They're going to make us fight," he said, indicating his escort with a tragic gesture. "They're taking us to the slaughter-house!"

They put us in a carriage and took us back to the inn to change. Calderón was so frightened that he could hardly get into his costume. Nervous and upset, he tried in vain to fashion the sash round his waist, meanwhile keeping up a flow of bitter reflections and lugubrious reminiscences.

"Bulls from this ranch," he muttered pessimistically, "put an end to So-and-so's bullfighting. They gored Whatsisname, and ripped his tripes out. They left Thingummybob six months in hospital, half-way between life and death. . . ."

Calderón's panic relieved some of my own. I finished my own dressing and joked with him while I helped him with his. We were marched through the streets to the bullring in full costume, surrounded by armed guards, and the howls and yells of the spectators when we did finally appear in the arena were ear-splitting. When the corrida started I was more frightened of the audience than I was of the bulls.

The first bull to come out was a huge beast with enormous horns; but contrary to our expectations it turned out to be brave and energetic. When it attacked the picadors they were not quick enough with their lances; and in a second, with two lightning rushes, it had the two horses belly upwards and was goring them furiously. The horses, the picadors, and an attendant who had been caught in the eruption formed a ghastly tangle which the bull ripped at again and again with its enormous horns. The butchery was horrible. We were paralysed with terror. Nobody knew what to do. The first man who detached himself from that shapeless and gory maelstrom of flesh was our friend the carter from the fish market, his face and hands streaming with blood, who galloped on all fours towards the barrera with an agility of which one would never have believed him capable.

This disastrous beginning had its natural result. Nobody felt like getting close to the bull. I made the best of the situation, opened my cape, and gave it a few passes as well as I could. There were no more horses and therefore no more *quites*, and when the time came for the kill the bull was as sound and strong as when it entered the ring. I gave it nine or ten passes with the muleta, and was lucky enough to catch it with a shallow thrust which dropped it. But the second bull to come out was horribly squint-eyed and proved wilder and more difficult. Since there were no more picadors, our banderilleros tried to punish it to some extent by stabbing it from the barrera whenever they had the chance. The public was ready to lynch us. I feigned a *quite*, and as I was making a *media verónica* the bull caught me and gored me in the leg.

They took me to the infirmary, which was really only a stable, and put me on a camp bed to attend to me. They had scarcely started to loosen my clothes when Paco Madrid was brought in with a wound in his arm. He also was deposited on the camp bed, which was the only one there was; and they were starting to look after us both when Calderón appeared, also wounded in the arm. And that was the end of the corrida. All three of us were piled into the tottering bed, and from there we heard the howling of the enraged multitude. Paco Madrid was cursing, Calderón was wailing, and I was yelling for somebody to look after us; and under the strain of our arguing and jumping about the bed gave way and deposited us all on the floor with a bone-shattering thud. Another banderillero, wounded both in the leg and arm at the same time, arrived to add himself to this scrambling heap of injured toreros; and meanwhile the public was threatening to set fire to the bullring and the Guardia Civil were shooting the bull which we had been unable to kill.

JUAN BELMONTE *Killer of Bulls*, trans. Leslie Charteris, 1937

THE DEAD TORERO

Such work can be the mischief of an hour.
This drunken-looking doll without a face
Was lovely Florentino. This was grace
And virtue smiling on the face of Power.

Shattered, that slim Toledo-tempered spine!
Hollow, the chrysalis, his gentle hand,
From which those wide imperial moths were fanned
Each in its hushed miraculous design!

He was the bee, with danger for his rose!
He died the sudden violence of Kings,
And from the bullring to the Virgin goes
Floating his cape. He has no need for wings.

ROY CAMPBELL

Customs and Idiosyncrasies

Spain is a land bottled up for antiquarians, and it must be confessed that the national process is very picturesque and classical.

RICHARD FORD

Ford was in fact talking about the sherry-making process, but what he says applies to most things Spanish. The most casual visitor continually sees the picturesque and classical. If you want to know what the life of your English village was like in the Middle Ages, don't try to imagine it among today's bungalows and red-brick villas but look at a Spanish village.

PEACE

"Here we are," said Pepe, and he rang a bell, suspended by the side of a broad gate.

"Who?" screeched a voice.

"Peace!" shouted Pepe. Never does one get such a clear sense of the medieval as when attempting to enter a Spanish house. Like a foraging warrior, one can pass through doors and gates only when one has pledged peace. Sometimes an eye will even gaze down from a hole in the ceiling, while the visitor shrinks instinctively to one side for fear of molten lead.

JOHN HAYCRAFT *Babel in Spain*

In *South from Granada* Gerald Brenan gives an account of the curious habits of the Andalusian village where he lived for many years. The first of the following passages describes the exact equivalent of the "rough music" of the Sussex village where I live, though here they use nothing so euphonic as cows' horns and conches but only old tin cans.

CENCERRADA AND PREGONES

One evening as I was sitting on the roof of my house I heard a deep muffled hooting like that of a railway shunter's horn, only much louder; it was gradually taken up by other horns in other parts of the village and from the hills round, till I felt besieged by an army of eerie and lugubrious sounds. On inquiring I was told that this was the *cencerrada* or charivari. When either a widow or widower announced their intention of getting married, the village lads went out with cows' horns and conches and blew on them. This was repeated every day with gradually increasing intensity for several weeks till the marriage took place. The unfortunate couple had also to suffer from *pregones*, a word which the dictionary translates as "public announcements". Young men and children would collect outside their houses and repeat verses, most of which would be obscene and scurrilous, warning them not to marry the other party. Here is an example of one of the more innocent:

> Don't you marry José
> for he is the father of misery.
> I spent a year with him
> and I passed that year in pain.
> All he ever gave me to eat
> was a dish of lentil pottage,
> a stale barley cake
> and a mess of hasty pudding.
> Then when we went hungry to bed
> he turned over and fell asleep.
> That's the sort of man he is—
> snores all night and wets the bed.
> Let the *cencerrada* go on.

THE MESA CAMILLA

This classic piece of furniture and the domestic rites accompanying it demand some explanation. Imagine then a circular deal table with a brazier of wood ash or charcoal set under it. Drape over it a red-flannel tablecloth that reaches on every side to the ground, and let three, four or six persons sit around it with the skirts of this tablecloth, which are split into sections, tucked about them. Let them have short coats or shawls thrown lightly over their backs and let their faces be leaning towards one another—either deep in a game of cards, or sewing, or else perfectly still and motionless, merely rippling the silence from time to time by some placid observation. Then you will have a picture of what family life is like during one half of the year in every town and village of this country.

It has sometimes occurred to me that one of the causes of the decline of Spain in the seventeenth century may have lain in this circular table. The forests were cut down, firewood became

A SPANISH BREAKFAST

*Lengths of batter fried in oil which the aficionado
takes to a café and dips in his coffee. That's all he
has till two-thirty, the normal Spanish lunch time*

A THIN COOL STREAM

Simple and sanitary: one porrón, *no glasses and you can have a party. The problem is to swallow with your mouth open*

scarce, the domestic idea spread, the men's habit of buttoning themselves up in cosy confabulation with their womenfolk—the wife's aunt, the mother, the elder children—instead of stretching their legs by the fire and leaving them to sit cross-legged on cushions in their *estrada*. Round the *mesa camilla* family life grew denser, thicker, more Orientally bourgeois: reading ceased in the prim harem atmosphere and the clubs or cafés—which till recent times were sordid, badly lit places—offered the only outlet and escape. Spain became the classic land of stagnation, the self-immersed Ottoman Empire of the West—a condition from which it did not finally emerge until the present century. The only people to gain were the engaged couples who, once the young man had been accepted and admitted to the house, could hold hands blissfully for hours at a time under the flannel tablecloth.

Anyone who has made the slightest contact with Spaniards in Spain, rich or poor, will know their proud generosity. I remember especially an evening in Ventas, a shabbily modern, totally unlovely suburb of Madrid near the new bullring, when it became quite impossible even to offer to pay for a drink. When they came to England, yes, maybe, but now we were in Spain, visitors and therefore guests.

A COMPLIMENT

On our arrival, we found the Bishop there, to whom I was presented, when he desired I might make the house my own, as both it and the gardens were at my service: and here I must observe to you, that this is a common Spanish compliment; for if a Spaniard's sword, watch, ring, or any thing else belonging to him be praised, he immediately offers it with warmth, though nothing would disappoint him more than to accept it.

MAJOR WILLIAM DALRYMPLE
Travels through Spain and Portugal in 1774

AN ANDALUSIAN BATH

To bathe is not unheard-of in Cordova, but bath tubs are completely unknown. In some places there exist huge jars, like those used by Ali Baba's forty thieves, and when anyone insists on taking a bath, such a jar is half filled with water. One gets in by climbing up and then down a double ladder, crouches down until only one's head protrudes through the neck of the jar, and can proceed to wash without interrupting one's conversation.

ALEXANDRE DUMAS *Paris to Cadiz*

If, in Spain, you have been reprimanded for exposing your arms in church, or more intimate parts on the beach, you should know that Spanish suspicion of the ways of Northern Europe is nothing new. When, at the treaty of Barcelona, Queen Isabel was said to have behaved immodestly, she wrote to her confessor.

SOME DANCED

You say that some danced who ought not to have danced; but if that is intended to convey that I danced, I can only say that it is not true; I have little custom of dancing, and I had no thought of such a thing. . . . The new masks you complain of were worn neither by me nor by my ladies; and not one dress was put on that had not been worn ever since we came to Aragon. The only dress I wore had, indeed, been seen by the Frenchmen before, and was my silk one with three bands of gold, made as plainly as possible. This was all my part of the festivity. Of the grand array and showy garments you speak of, I saw nothing and knew nothing until I read your letter. The visitors who came may have worn such fine things when they appeared; but I know of no others. As for the French people supping with the ladies at table, that is a thing they are accustomed to do. They do not get the custom from us; but when their guests dine with sovereigns, the others in their train dine at tables in the hall with the ladies and gentlemen; and there are no separate tables for ladies. The Burgundians, the English and the Portuguese, also follow this custom; and we on similar occasions to this. So there is no more evil in it, nor bad repute, than in asking guests to your own table. I say this, that you may see that there was no innovation in what we did.

FATHER FLOREZ *Reinas Católicos*

COURT ETIQUETTE—1804

Much talk about ye etiquette and ceremonial of the Sp. Court. King and Q., and even the little *Infantes*, served with drink by the gentlemen-in-waiting on their knees. Old custom retained of tasting what the King is to drink and eat. When the cup is carried through the apartments or corridors of the palace, every one by whom it passes must take off his hat. At the Escorial once lately an obstinate fellow refused, upon which the bearer of the cup threw it down, with the exclamation of "Copa profanada"; the man was imprisoned for the insult. Duty of the gentlemen-in-waiting excessively hard. There are 12. . . . Scratch King's back at night when he is in bed. Gives water, etc., *par extraordinaire,* but not since English improvements have been introduced. *Sumiller de cuerpo* (Lord Chamberlain) puts on K.'s shirt. Forms observed when K. is sick, even continued after his death. "No quiere comer el Rey?" ("Does not the King wish to eat?") till he is interred, when the *Sumiller* breaks his wand or staff of office, and exclaims with surprise, "Esta muerto el Rey?"

The Spanish Journal of Elizabeth Lady Holland

Bullfighting (and football) are not the only Spanish sports.

A FAVOURITE GAME IN BISCAY

Every evening while I remained in Bilbao, I spent half an hour in the Swiss Coffee-house—the only one in the town; and one evening, I was much amused by a very curious scene I witnessed there. Four gentlemen were seated at a card-table when I entered the coffee-house, and at first I paid no particular attention to them; but accidentally resting my eye upon them while sipping my coffee, I was surprised to see one of the players shut one eye, and at the same time thrust his tongue out of his mouth; from him, my eyes wandered to another, who at the same moment squinted with both eyes, and thrust forward his under-lip: I now saw that it was a constant succession of face-making, while all the while the game went on. It is impossible to describe the strange, ludicrous, and hideous faces of the players; I was at first dumb with astonishment, and then convulsed with laughter, and all the while dying with curiosity to know the reason of so grotesque an exhibition. It was a Biscayan game, called *mūs;*—answering to each card there is a particular contortion of the face, which interprets its value; and the point of the game consists in the dexterity with which partners are able to convey to each other by grimaces, the state of each other's hand. This is a favourite game in Biscay, but it is said to require a lifetime to become expert in it.

HENRY D. INGLIS Spain in 1830

PELOTA

All the year round the historic Basque game of pelota is played at the Jai Alai or great court near the Calle del Carmen. The game itself is very fine; it puts the well-grown, white-clad bodies of the young Basque pelotaris into splendid play, which has perhaps had more to do with its great success in Paris than its purely sporting interest. It is played by sides of two or three in a three-walled court, consisting of one side and two end walls, of which the side wall is almost three times as long as the others. The fourth side is occupied by a gallery for spectators. The ball is about the size of a tennis-ball, but hard, and is struck against one of the end walls with a large, narrow, spoon-shaped wicker glove, known as the cesta. Rules and scoring are not unlike those of racquets, and are very easily understood.

The moment play begins a gang of desperate looking ruffians starts calling out the odds, which are taken freely by the audience. The bookmakers stand in the court and throw the tickets up to the backers in the gallery in pierced tennis-balls, into which the backers put their stakes and toss them back. The odds often take dizzy runs while the fifty points which are usually played are being scored; experienced backers often manage to get odds both ways. For instance, the betting having opened at evens, after fifteen minutes' play the score may stand at: Blues, 15; Reds, 5. Fifty minutes later Reds have scored 35, and Blues only 20. Wild excitement, especially if there is a dark horse on either side. Has Blues' opening run exhausted them? The bookmakers are evidently not all in the know, for widely different views of the situation are betrayed by the varying odds offered. Now is the time for the careful punter, who has put three dollars on Reds at ten to three early in the day, to make sure of the thing by taking the proffered seven to four the other way.

The very mixed audience cheers its colour for a good return, curses it for a bad one, and wildly applauds an error on the other side. The bookies keep up a deafening roar. The air is thick with blasphemy, tobacco smoke, and sweltering humanity. Grim, heavily moustachioed old ladies sit in deepest black, pencil and paper in hand, not letting a move of the game, or of the betting, escape them. They know every pelotari in the court, and long experience has taught them to catch that indefinable atmosphere which lingers about a queer game, and to turn the knowledge to account. In the meantime Blues have scored a little, but Reds move steadily forward. Gradually the betting droops; no one will take six to one. Reds have only five or six points more to make, and Blues are a dozen behind. The pelotaris are tired, one or two of them dead beat. The crowd has stopped its cheers and curses, and those who have no money to touch take themselves off. Now and then a hideously raucous bookmaker screeches out some absurd odds which no one dreams of taking. And the match ends, rather less bravely than it began.

ROYALL TYLER *Spain: Her Life and Arts*, 1909

Cockfighting is against the law today, but you can still see it if you're lucky—or unlucky. If you do, it's best to make sure that there's a Guardia Civil in the audience. This Italian writer advised his readers to "be content, humane people, with the sight of the bulls".

A MADRID COCK FIGHT

When I entered, there were a hundred persons present. What kind of people are these? I asked of myself. And really the audience of the cock-circus resembles that of no other theatre; it is a mixture, *sui generis*, which is only to be seen at Madrid. There are no women, boys, soldiers, nor workmen, because it is a work-day and an inconvenient hour; yet, nevertheless, one notices there a greater variety of faces, dresses, and attitudes than in any other public gathering. They are all people who have nothing to do the entire day long; they are comedians, with long hair and bald heads; *toreros* (Calderon, the famous *picador*, was there) with their red sashes around their waists; students, bearing on their faces the traces of a night passed at gambling; cock merchants, elegant young men, old gentlemen amateurs, dressed in black, with black gloves and large cravats . . . all of whom know each other, and discuss, in one voice among themselves, the quality of the cocks which have been announced in the programme of the spectacle, the wagers of the preceding day, the accidents of the combat, the claws, feathers, spurs, wings, beaks, and wounds, making use of the very rich terminology of the art, and citing rules, examples, cocks of former times, famous struggles, winnings, and losses.

The spectacle began at the appointed hour . . . the president took his place, the secretary cried, *Silencio!*—the weigher and another servant each took a box, and placing them at the opposite gates on the railing, opened them together. The cocks came out, the gates were closed, and the spectators preserved a profound silence for some moments.

They were two *Andalusian cocks of English breed*, to make use of the curious definition given me by one of the spectators. They were tall, slender, straight as arrows, with a long and very flexible neck, completely without feathers behind, and from the chest up; they had no crest, a small head, and a pair of eyes which revealed their warlike character. The spectators look at them without a word. The aficionados (amateurs) in those few moments judge from the colour, shape, and movement of the two which one will probably be the victor; then offer their wagers. It is a judgement, as any one can understand, which is very uncertain at best; but it is just this uncertainty which gives life to the affair; suddenly the silence is broken by a burst of shouts:

Un duro (a crown) *for the right one! A crown for the left one!*

*Done! Three crowns for the dark one! Four crowns for the grey one!
Una onza* (eighty lire) *for the little one! Done!* etc. . . .

The two cocks do not look at each other from the beginning.
One is turned in one direction, the other in another; they crow,
stretching out their necks towards the spectators, as if they
were asking, "What do you wish?" Little by little, without
giving any signs of having seen each other, they approach; it
seems as if each wished to take the other by surprise. Suddenly,
as quickly as a flash, they take a leap with outstretched wings,
strike in the air, and fall back, shedding a cloud of feathers
around them. After the first blow, they stop, and plant themselves opposite each other, with their necks outstretched and
their beaks nearly touching, looking fixedly at each other, and
quite motionless, as if they wished to poison one another with
their eyes. Then they dash at each other again violently, after
which the assaults succeed each other without any interruption. They wound with their claws, spurs, and beaks; they
clasp each other with their wings, so that they look like one
cock with two heads; they each dash under the other's breast,
beat against the iron railing, chase each other, fall, slip, and fly;
little by little, the blows fall more thickly, more feathers fly
from their heads, their necks become flame-color, and they lose
blood. Then they begin beating each other with their heads,
around the eyes, in the eyes; they tear each other's flesh with
the fury of two demoniacs who are afraid of being separated.
It seems as if they knew that one of them must die; they utter
no sound, not even a groan; nothing is heard but the noise of
rustling wings, of breaking feathers, of beaks which are hitting
bone; and there is not an instant's truce; it is a fury which ends
only in death.

The spectators follow intently all these movements with
their eyes, they count the fallen feathers, number the wounds,
and the shouting becomes more exciting, and the wagers larger:

*Five crowns for the little one! Eight crowns for the grey one!
Twenty crowns for the dark one! Done! Done!*

At a certain point, one of the two cocks makes a movement
that betrays the inferiority of his strength, and begins to give
signs of weariness. While still holding out, the blows of the
beak become fewer, its clawings weaker, and its leaps lower; it
seems to understand that it must die; it does not fight to kill,
but not to be killed; it recedes, flees, falls, rises, returns only
to fall again, and totters as if seized with giddiness. Then the
spectacle becomes horrible. In the presence of the enemy, who
is surrendering, the victor grows more ferocious; its peckings
fall thick and fast and pitilessly into the eyes of its victim,
with the regularity of a sewing machine. . . . There is something
of the convict, keeper, executioner about it; it appears to be

saying something in the ear of its victim, and seems to accompany every blow with an insult. There, take that, suffer, die, no! live, take this, and this, and this! A little of its sanguinary rage takes possession of you; that cowardly cruelty awakens in you a mania for revenge; you would gladly strangle it with your hands, or crush it with your feet. The conquered cock, all covered with blood, featherless and tottering, attempts an assault from time to time, gives several pecks, flees, and dashes itself against the iron railing to seek a mode of escape.

Those who are betting grow more excited and shout louder. They can no longer bet on the struggle, so they bet on the agony:

Five crowns that it does not make three more attacks! Three crowns that it does not make five! Four crowns that it does not make two! Done! Done!

At this point I heard a voice which made me shudder: *Es ciego* (it is blind). . . .

The dying cock slowly raised its head; the brutal victor, quite ready, overwhelmed it with a shower of blows. The shouts burst out again; the victim made another slight movement, was hit again, shook itself, received another blow still, blood issued from its mouth, it tottered and fell. The cowardly victor began to crow. A servant comes and carries both of them away.

All the spectators rose and began a noisy conversation; the winners laughing loudly, the losers swearing; both parties discussing the merits of the cocks and incidents of the fight. *A good fight! Good cocks! Bad cocks! They are worth nothing! You do not understand it, sir! Good! Bad!*

Be seated, gentlemen! shouted the president; all sat down and another fight began.

EDMONDO DE AMICIS *Spain and the Spaniards*, 1881

HIS CIGAR

But whether at bull-fight or theatre, be he lay or clerical, every Spaniard who can afford it, consoles himself continually with a cigar, sleep—not bed—time only excepted.

RICHARD FORD *Gatherings from Spain*

Spain is a land of proverbs. There is at least one for every occasion, and every Spanish conversation is full of them.

PROVERBS

El huésped y el pez, a dos días huelen.
"Guests and fish smell after two days."

Menda y mangue grasté, os dui terablamos manguelo yequé.
"Both my horse and I have a petition to make."

Gypsy request

En tierra de ciegos, el tuerto es rey.
"In the land of the blind the one-eyed is king."

Da Dios nueces al que no tiene muelas.
"God gives nuts to the toothless."

La mujer y el melón, bien maduritos.
"A woman and a melon, let them be fairly ripe."

Quien con perros se acuesta con pulgas se levanta.
"He who sleeps with dogs wakes up with fleas."

La mentira y la torta, gorda.
"A cake and a lie, let them be big."

Los muertos en la huesa, y los vivos a la mesa.
"The dead to their graves, the living to their dinners."

Por dinero baila el perro.
"For money the dog dances."

El amor es fuego, pero con él no se cuece el puchero.
"Love is a furnace but it will not cook the stew."

Dios es el que sana, ye el medico lleva la plata.
"God cures the patient and the doctor pockets the fee."

Dios es omnipotente, y el dinero es su teniente.
"God is omnipotent and money is his lieutenant."

*Si tu mujer quiere que te tires de un balcón, pide a Dios que
   sea bajo.*
"If your wife tells you to throw yourself from a balcony, pray
   God that it's a low one."

Food and Drink

En el sur se fríe, en el centro se asa y en el norte se guisa.
"In the south they fry, in the centre they roast and in the north
they stew."

Spanish saying

Solo hay dos clases de vino de Jerez, el bueno y el mejor.
"There are only two kinds of sherry, the good and the better."

Jerez saying

To appreciate Spanish food you must like olive oil and
garlic, and like them a lot. Provided you do, it is
tastier, and more varied than the food of any other
Mediterranean country—and in my opinion than that
of any country in Europe, except France. But it has a
bad reputation.

PUCHERO, NATIONAL DISH OF CASTILE

This is a boiled affair, not unlike the French *pot-au-feu*, of
which the essential ingredients are pork, chunks of *tocino* or
bacon fat, potatoes, turnips and chick peas. The chick pea . . .
is a yellow bullet which explodes in the inside into several cubic
feet of gas, while if the cook knows her job properly she will
see that the meat is boiled till it has no taste left and that the
fat, a yellowish white in colour, is rancid. A Spaniard feels
when he eats this dish that he has vindicated his toughness of
fibre. He has not degenerated from the breed of men who
conquered a continent with a handful of adventurers, wore
hair-shirts day and night till they stuck to their flesh, and
braved the mosquitoes of the Pilcomayo and the Amazon.

GERALD BRENAN South from Granada

IN SPAYNE

Al your wyne shalbe kepte and caryed in gote skyns, & the
here syde shalbe inwarde, and you shall draw your wyne out
of one of the legges of the skyne. whan you go to dyner & to

supper, you must fetch your bread in one place, and your wyne in a nother place, and your meate in a nother place; & hogges in many places shalbe vnder your feete at the table, and lice in your bed.

DR ANDREW BOORDE
The Fyrst Boke of the Introduction of Knowledge

And in the south things become still cruder.

MIGAS

A sort of porridge, but fried in olive oil, garlic and water. It could be made either of wheat or maize flour or of breadcrumbs. The poor eat it with the invariable sardines, the cheapest and dullest of the Mediterranean fishes and often the only one to reach our village, while the rich like to pour hot chocolate over it. My landlord . . . took it with both chocolate and fried fish, stirred up well together.

GERALD BRENAN *South from Granada*

As in everything else, Richard Ford took a lively and analytical interest in Spanish food.

GAZPACHO

Any remarks on Spanish salads would be incomplete without some account of *gazpacho*, that vegetable soup, or floating salad, which during the summer forms the food of the bulk of the people in the torrid portions of Spain. This dish is of Arabic origin, as its name, "soaked bread", implies. This most ancient Oriental Roman and Moorish refection is composed of onions, garlic, cucumbers, chilis, all chopped up very small and mixed together with crumbs of bread, then put into a bowl of oil, vinegar, and fresh water. Reapers and agricultural labourers could never stand the sun's fire without this cooling acetous diet. . . .

In Andalucia, during the summer, a bowl of gazpacho is commonly ready in every house of an evening, and is partaken of by every person who comes in. It is not easily digested by strangers, who do not require it quite so much as the natives, whose souls are more parched and dried up, and who perspire less.

Gatherings from Spain

FISH OR WOMEN

*En los meses que no tienen erre
ni pescado ni mujeres.*

"In months which have no R
don't take fish or women."

Andalusian saying

OF CAPONS

The capons are very fat. Their method of fattening them is by giving a walnut with the shell every day, increasing the number to forty, at which time they are reckoned to be in a state of perfection.

The Spanish Journal of Elizabeth Lady Holland

Capons do hang their stones about their necks that they may be admired.

The Tangier Papers of Samuel Pepys

Very good table wines are made in Spain, particularly in the Rioja district, but it is for the sherry of Jerez that Spain is rightly famous. Of the many different sherries and similar wines my favourite is Manzanilla—the one of which you can drink most.

MANZANILLA—AND ALPISTERA

The natives of Xerez themselves infinitely prefer a light wine called Manzanilla, which is made near San Lucar, and is at once much weaker and cheaper than sherry. The grape from whence it is produced grows on a poor and sandy soil. The vintage is very early, as the fruit is gathered before it is quite ripe. The wine is of a delicate pale straw colour, and is extremely wholesome; it strengthens the stomach, without heating or inebriating, like sherry. All classes are passionately fond of it, since the want of alcohol enables them to drink more of it than of stronger beverages, while the dry quality acts as a tonic during the relaxing heats. . . . The men employed in the sherry wine vaults, and who have therefore that drink at their command, seldom touch it, but invariably, when their work is done, go to the neighbouring shop to refresh themselves with a glass of "innocent" Manzanilla. Among their betters, clubs are formed solely to drink it, and with iced water and a cigar it transports the consumer into a Moslem's dream of paradise. . . .

The origin of the name has been disputed; some who prefer sound to sense derive it from *manzana*, an apple, which had it been cider might have passed; others connect it with the distant town of *Mansanilla* on the opposite side of the river, where it is neither made nor drunk. The real etymology is to be found in its striking resemblance to the bitter flavour of the flowers of camomile (*manzanilla*), which are used by our doctors to make a medicinal tea, and by those of Spain for fomentations. This flavour in the wine is so marked as to be at first quite disagreeable to strangers. If its eulogistic consumers are to be believed, the wine surpasses the tea in hygaeian qualities: none, say they, who drink it are ever troubled with gravel, stone, or gout. . . .

By the way, the real thing to eat with Manzanilla is the *alpistera*. Make it thus:—To one pound of fine flour (mind that it is dry) add half a pound of double-refined, well sifted, pounded white sugar, the yolks and whites of four very fresh eggs, well beaten together; work the mixture up into a paste; roll it out very thin; divide it into squares about half the size of this page; cut it into strips, so that the paste should look like a hand with fingers; then dislocate the strips, and dip them in hot melted fine lard, until of a delicate pale brown; the more the strips are curled up and twisted the better; the *alpistera* should look like bunches of ribbons; powder them over with fine white sugar. They are then as pretty as nice.

RICHARD FORD *Gatherings from Spain*

From Falstaff's time sherry has been an Englishman's drink.

SHERRIS-SACK

A good sherris-sack hath a two-fold operation in it. It ascends me into the brain; dries me there all the foolish and dull and crudy vapours which environ it; makes it apprehensive, quick, forgetive, full of nimble fiery and delectable shapes; which deliver'd o'er to the voice, the tongue, which is the birth, becomes excellent wit. The second property of your excellent sherris is, the warming of the blood; which, before cold and settled, left the liver white and pale, which is the badge of pusillanimity and cowardice; but the sherris warms it and makes it course from the inwards to the parts extreme. It illumineth the face, which, as a beacon, gives warning to all the rest of this little kingdom, man, to arm; and then the vital commoners and inland petty spirits muster me all to their captain, the heart, who, great and puffed up with this retinue, doth any deed of courage; and this valour comes of sherris. So that skill in the weapon is nothing without sack, for it sets it a-work; and learning, a mere hoard of gold kept by a devil till sack commences it and sets it in act and use. Hereof comes it that Prince Harry is valiant; for the cold blood he did inherit of his father, he hath, like lean, sterile, and bare land, manured, husbanded, and tilled, with excellent endeavour of drinking good and good store of fertile sherris, that he is become very hot and valiant. If I had a thousand sons, the first human principle I would teach them should be, to forswear thin potations and to addict themselves to sack.

WILLIAM SHAKESPEARE

Sherry is made by the *solera* process. There are no vintage sherries because the wine of one year is blended a little at a time with earlier wines. The treading is traditional.

THE TREADING

Imagine a wooden trough or manger which, instead of being long and narrow, is about ten foot square. It is raised a yard above the ground and slightly tilted so that its smooth wooden floor is on an incline from the wall behind it to the front of the *lagar*. This, of course, is to allow the grape juice to run forward to the small spout from which a conduit takes it to the vat standing ready before it, from which it will be poured into the barrel. In the centre of the *lagar* rises the press which is exactly like one of those old-fashioned paper presses once seen in solicitors' offices, but about seven foot high.

When the grapes are brought in from the *almijar* outside, two or four men are standing in each *lagar*. The *lagares* are not isolated structures but are in rows, perhaps as many as half a dozen running down one wall of the building. These men, the *pisadores* or "treaders", are armed each with a kind of spade made entirely of wood. They wear nothing but a shirt, shorts and specially studded boots of cow-hide called *zapatos de pisar*. These have cross rows and an edging of nails protruding and are made in this way so that while the juice of the grape is squeezed out by treading, the pips remain with the skin and stalk and, eluding the nails, are unbroken. The Jerezanos claim that these boots are more effective than the naked feet.

It is now midnight. The building in which the *lagares* stand is cool and dim for we are in an isolated house, probably, a mile from the road and beyond even the all-pervading electricity system of Spain. The midnight hours have been chosen because if the grapes are pressed when it is cool the must is less likely to start fermenting prematurely.

The scene is theatrical. The bare-legged *pisadores* armed with their wooden shovels, like giant children's spades from the seaside, the golden-green grapes, the rich vinous musty smell of the liquor that has already run into the butts, the dark serious faces—for hilarity will only come in sudden bursts when the *pisadores* are tired and have drunk some of the wine to which they are entitled without stint—the air of tension, almost of devoutness as though this ancient rite were still, as once it was, religious. Then the beginning of movement in the *lagares*, the rhythmic quickstep with which the fruit is pressed. . . .

The solemnity of the treaders is characteristic of this people, even when, very rarely, they sing "slow old tunes of Spain" to their quick fatiguing dance-steps. They are intent and humorous rather than frivolously mirthful. This is a hard task and the *pisadores* will work from midnight to midday without showing weariness or ill-humour, but they work with dignity and song, never ceasing their rhythmic double mark-time, their choruses are full of flamenco spirit rather than dithyrambic hysteria.

RUPERT CROFT-COOKE *Sherry*, 1955

The trade with England has had its ups and downs. Best known was the famous "plastering" scandal in the late nineteenth century. In the process of making sherry, gypsum (calcium sulphate) is added and this was said to produce a harmful proportion of sulphuric acid in the drink. In 1872 a Dr J. L. W. Thudichum, M.D., published a violent attack on sherry. A defender suggested that he was less than an impartial observer.

THEIR DAILY PINT

In common candour, the author of this incredible misrepresentation ought not to have withheld from the public his qualifications to speak so confidently on the subject. He should have told them that he had visited Jerez under the auspices of certain shipping houses to whom he offered, if not to repeat the miracle of Cana, at any rate to produce amontillado by purely chemical agency—that he was provided with considerable funds for the purchase of scientific instruments which he was incompetent to use, and that he resided in Jerez in style for a period of three months at the expense of his principal patron, during which time he lost him half his vineyard's produce through the so-called amontillado which he professed to fabricate, turning out such vile stuff that it could only be employed for rinsing the casks with, while a further experiment which he made in the bodega of a second shipper resulted in transforming the wine into vinegar.

The public, knowing nothing of the motive which prompted these attacks upon sherry, naturally grew alarmed, and for a time the subject formed a common topic at all dinner-tables, where by the lady at your side you found sherry generally declined with thanks. Middle-aged gentlemen, too, perfectly hale and hearty on their daily pint of sherry, fancied that perhaps for them a day of reckoning might be near.

HENRY VIZETELLY *Facts about Sherry*

The public continued to be alarmed about what sherry would do to its liver till eventually *The Lancet* sent a Mr Vasey to investigate. In October 1898 it published his findings.

OUR COMMISSIONER

Our commissioner visited most of the large bodegas in Jerez, San Lucar, and Montilla, where sherry-growing is carried out on a gigantic scale. He was met with the greatest courtesy by the sherry-growers—and three-fourths of the industry is carried on by English people—and every step in the interesting processes was shown to him. . . . There are two facts in connexion with the production of sherry which are open to be construed as adulteration. The first is the addition of sulphate of lime to the crushed grapes before fermentation and the second the addition of a small proportion of spirit to wine intended for export. Against the former we do not think that a rational objection can be raised so long as the treatment is kept within limits, and this is invariably so. It may be called an artificial recourse, but so also is the adding of sugar-candy to champagne to make it sparkling or of gelatine, clay, and so on for the purpose of refining wines, beers, etc. We have described how the same thing may be to some extent naturally effected by the simple occurrence of an unusual proportion of vineyard dust adhering to the grapes prior to pressing. We venture to suggest that this has been the origin of the so-called "plastering process". The sulphate of lime employed is a natural constituent of the soil contiguous to the vineyards. The question is, can this be regarded in the light of adulteration or fraud, since it does not add in any way to the bulk of the wine nor does it make it poisonous? On the contrary, it refines the wine and increases its power to develop those fragrant ethers which give to the wine its peculiarly pleasant characters in regard to bouquet, flavour, and agreeable stimulating qualities.

Drink, and wine in particular, gathers more misinformation, superstition and prejudice than most other subjects, and sherry has not escaped. For example the English opinion that sherry is a before-dinner drink.

FOR DINNER

Manzanilla will carry you nearly through dinner, and others of the lighter class will go all through, though they may not be drinkable in quite such volume. I once even attempted a fully graded *menu* and wine-list with sherry only to fill the latter—a "sherry dinner" to match the claret feasts often given by lovers of the Gascon wine. It was before I began to keep such documents, and so I am not quite certain of the details. But if I were reconstructing such an entertainment now, and had the wherewithal as I once had, I should arrange it somewhat thus: Manzanilla with oysters; Montilla with soup and fish; an Amontillado with entrées and roast; an Amoroso or some such wine with sweets; and for after dinner, the oldest and brownest of "old Browns."

GEORGE SAINTSBURY *Notes on a Cellar-Book*, 1920

Or the English opinion that any sherry will keep indefinitely in an open bottle or decanter.

IN THE BOTTLE

A delicate, unsweetened fino begins to deteriorate immediately. There is an excellent fino sherry, widely sold in public houses, that is often abused for being below standard, or for not being as good as it used to be. The brewers buy it in bulk; then they store it in warm warehouses for a year or two; then they send it to the publican, who keeps it for another year or two before he opens it in a bar as hot as a furnace; the bottle is left open for weeks, and then the wine is served in the wrong glasses, and some perspicacious customer complains that it is imperfect. The bottle may or may not then be returned with a stiff letter to the long-suffering shipper. The wine does not stand a chance. . . .

Once the bottle has been opened, fino sherry gets coarse very quickly: the more delicate the wine, the more noticeable this is. Professor Saintsbury said that he could notice the difference between lunch time and dinner. A natural fino should be drunk within three days of opening the bottle.

PEASANT WOMEN AND DONKEY

*Symbols of Spain today, met on every road, seen in the streets
of every town and village. Picturesque for the tourist, but
how much longer will a country which was once the most
powerful in the world be able to stay in the Middle Ages?*

FOR GRAPES AND PILGRIMS

It is the time of the grape harvest in Puente la Reina in the Rioja wine district. Through this small town in northern Spain ran the route to Santiago, and on its narrow, unpaved bridge you can get a good idea of the long hard pilgrimage this must have been

Or the confident way in which sherry is usually served in "sherry" glasses.

IN THE GLASS

Sherris-sack was first drunk from silver vessels—and they usually held a man's measure. Then, during the seventeenth century, Venetian glass was introduced into England, and sherry was generally drunk from flute glasses. A very wide choice of wine glasses is available today; many of them are aesthetically very beautiful; hardly any are suitable for drinking wine out of, and the so-called "sherry glasses" are by far the worst of all. One of the most beautiful things about sherry is its deep, penetrating fragrance that prepares the palate to receive the flavour of the wine; the bouquet of a good sherry is so attractive that one can enjoy it without tasting the wine at all. If it is served in a public house sherry glass, all that is lost, and the beauty of a really good sherry is destroyed. Such a wine needs a big glass with plenty of room for the full fragrance to gather within it. Tulip-shaped wine glasses only filled half-way are very good, but the special tall tasting glasses used in the wine trade are still better. These are from three to six inches high and gently taper towards the top; they should only be filled to the height of an inch or so.

JULIAN JEFFS *Sherry*, 1961

Travellers in Spain

There is a good deal of Spain that has not been perambulated.
I would have you go thither.

DR JOHNSON to Boswell

In spite of Dr Johnson's advice, it is only for about the
last sixty years that Spain has been thought really safe
to visit. It was far too dangerous and uncivilized to be
on the grand tour circuit. As Dr Andrew Boorde said,
he would rather go five times to Rome. Even in the
eighteenth century it must have been the equivalent
of going today, uninoculated, to tropical Africa. And
when illnesses seemed less likely, Spanish robbers
replaced them.

HEADS

Not far from this *venta*, to the right of the road, stood some
pillars on which the heads of three or four malefactors were
exposed to view: this is always a reassuring sight, and proves
that one is in a civilized country.

THÉOPHILE GAUTIER *Un Voyage en Espagne*

But it was only with the coming of D.D.T. that travel in
Spain became at all comfortable. I remember noticing
this dramatic change between late 1951 and early 1953.

THE TRAVELLER'S REPOSE

The repose of the traveller is disturbed in the smaller Spanish
towns by the hourly cry of the *sereno* or night-watchman. Other
enemies of repose (most troublesome in the N.W.) may be
repelled by Persian or Keating's insect powder, a supply of
which should be brought from England.

BAEDEKER'S *Spain and Portugal*, 1908

There were times when you travelled, like an army,
with your baggage train.

170

We hope, on our return, to present you with a complete collection of the best wines in Spain; travelling with such a waggon-load of things, a few bottles more or less are not felt; we are obliged to carry, not only our beds, but bread, wine, meat, oil, and salt, from one great town to another; for we seldom meet with any thing in the inns but bare walls, and perhaps a few eggs, which are sold at an unconscionable price. If we chance to find a few unbroken chairs, we esteem ourselves uncommonly fortunate; yet it is astonishing how dear travelling is in this country. As much is asked for giving you house-room, as would purchase a good supper and lodgings in the best inns, in most other parts of Europe. As our health is excellent, and consequently our spirits good, we are easily reconciled to these kinds of hardships. . . . The mildness of the climate obviates all inconveniences that might accrue from a total want of glass, or even paper, in the windows; or of a door or shutter that can be fastened close enough to keep wind or rain out.

As soon as we arrive at one of these barns, called Ventas, our first care is to set up our beds. The kitchen is generally at one end; the mules stand in the back part, and our apartment is a partition run up against the wall to the street, with a hole or two for light, defended by three or four very useless iron bars, for a pigmy could not squeeze through the window.

Next our cook takes his stand at the hearth, to warm our broth, which we carry, ready made, in a kettle behind our chaise; and if he can procure fuel and elbow-room, tosses up a hash, or some such campaign dish. Sometimes we are lucky enough to have an opportunity of setting our spit, or broiling a chop upon our gridiron; but these luxuries we are not to expect above once or twice in the course of a week.

While our repast is preparing, we read, draw, or write, by the light of a long brass lamp. Our supper dispatched, and a bottle of wine placed between us, we enjoy an hour's merry chat, to give the servants time to sup, and then we retire to bed, where we lie very snug till the dawn. . . .

This morning, on leaving Girona, we met with a laughable accident. S. G. who travels in the vehicle of the mountebank, was roused from his nap by the bottom of the chaise suddenly giving way, and dropping them both into the river Ter. They were obliged to walk in the chaise . . . quite through the water, before their horses could be prevailed upon to stop.

HENRY SWINBURNE *Travels through Spain*, 1779

171

By early Victorian times things had improved, and there was a choice of methods.

BY COACH

Our vehicle was drawn by eight mules, sometimes by ten. Their coats, thickening for winter, had been clipped along their backs only, and as one looked down on them they seemed just like huge rats harnessed to a fairy coach. They were handled by a team of three men, the *mayoral*, corresponding to our coachman, the *sotacochero*, or postilion, and the *zagal*, for whom there is no equivalent in any language. The *zagal* seems scarcely human. He jumps on and off the coach like a monkey; bounds along like a tiger; like a demon he hounds his team with sticks, a whip, even stones. His official station is a little platform on the front of the coach, near the driver, but he is never there. He canters, gallops with the mules, yelling encouragement or a stream of profanities. When they run flat out, so does he. If they bolt he heads them off and catches them. A coach without its *zagal* is just a coach. With him it is an eagle pursuing a cloud, the wind that follows a whirlwind. Never shall I understand why the coach does not shake to pieces or overturn. . . .

Even if the coach does not capsize, it bounces high in the air at least twice before it can settle steadily on all four wheels again. Can you imagine the passengers? All unaware that they are nearing such a hole, they are dozing, chatting, lounging on the cushions, relaxing as best they can. Suddenly comes the first jolt; passengers, firearms, travelling bags are all hurled up to the roof, bruising and damaging each other, and at a conservative estimate there are four such holes per mile. Certainly the *mayoral* could avoid them and spare his passengers all these involuntary leaps and somersaults if he would slacken speed to a trot, but the Spanish postilion must always drive at full gallop to maintain his reputation, so trees and houses fly past and the very skyline rushes along like some fantastic streamer.

ALEXANDRE DUMAS *Paris to Cadiz*

BY DILIGENCE

Now that the royal monopoly is broken down, many new competing companies have sprung up; this mode of travelling is the cheapest and safest, nor is it thought at all beneath the dignity of "the best set", nay royalty itself goes by coach. Thus the Infante Don Francisco de Paula constantly hires the whole diligence to convey himself and his family from Madrid to the sea-coast; and one reason gravely given for Don Enrique's not coming to marry the Queen, was that his Royal Highness could not get a place, as the dilly was booked full.

RICHARD FORD *Gatherings from Spain*

And, of course, when these early travellers came home they all wrote books.

WHAT THEY WROTE

When I got home, I fell to reading the other books, the learned books and the tourist books, the intelligent books and the silly books, the critical books and the gushing books, so that now I know about the tourists of all periods in Iberia. I was pleased to note that a great number of them, both British and French, had been stoned by the Spanish, as well as stared at. I was pleased not from malice but from pride, for I had myself only been stared and shouted at, except for a few boys on the ramparts of Peñiscola who had thrown down two or three harmless tomatoes at me, which I thought moderate from a notoriously xenophobe people. Actually, I encountered much friendliness.

But what I mainly found peculiar in the nineteenth-century tourists was the extreme interest many of them displayed in the personal appearance of the female Spaniards, who always seem to me to be among the less interesting objects in any landscape. I mean, of course, not especially the female Spaniards (who are usually handsome) but the human population of any country. This is, no doubt, my personal limitation of taste, which finds buildings and landscape more aesthetically pleasing than the animal creation. But many visitors to Spain seem to have been almost as much interested in gazing at females as are the Spanish themselves: they are for ever darting, with an ardour almost Byronic, after bright eyes and flirted fans, and delight to compare the complexions, shapes and walks of ladies all over the peninsula. Indeed the ladies, and also the gentlemen, look very well, and much better than most ladies and gentlemen elsewhere, except in Italy; but still less well than the curve of a little fishing port round a crescent beach, or the golden stone baroque façade of a Romanesque church, or the palm-grown plaza of some small white tile-domed town, or the sweep of a pastel-hued mountainside up from a blue bay to the ruined citadel on its crest, or a terraced garden of olives, oranges and figs sprawling sweetly round an ancient sun-baked farm built in the great apse of a long-abandoned convent or church. It is these things, and a thousand more, that make the exquisiteness and poetry of Spain. But let the susceptible nineteenth-century tourist catch sight of a shapely female form, and all the glories of landscape and architecture were forgotten.

ROSE MACAULAY Fabled Shore

Twelve years ago, when I went by boat to Palma, there was one blocked lavatory for two hundred deck passengers, and in the night I lost overboard one half of the only silk pyjamas I have ever owned (I was using them for a pillow). Today I'm sure it is much more comfortable. When George Sand crossed with Chopin, who was already ill with consumption, things were worse.

BY BOAT TO PALMA

It was therefore entirely thanks to the hog that I could visit the island; had I entertained the idea of going there three years before, the prospect of so long and hazardous a journey by coaster would have made me abandon it. But, with the export of hogs, civilization has made its impression on Majorca. A handsome little steamer was bought in England which, though not built to defy the dreadful north winds that blow in Balearic waters, yet, when the weather is calm, weekly conveys two hundred pigs to Barcelona, and a few passengers as well.

It is pleasant to watch with what tender solicitude these gentlemen (I am not referring to the passengers) are treated on board, and how affectionately they are put ashore. The captain of the steamer is a most agreeable man who, as a result of living and conversing with such noble creatures, has adopted their exact vocal tones and even some of their unselfconsciousness. If a passenger complains of the noise they make, the captain tells him that it is the sound of minted gold rolling on the counter. If a woman is squeamish enough to notice the stench that pervades the ship, a husband is there to remind her that money smells pretty good and that, without hogs, she would have no silk dresses, no French hats, no Barcelonese mantillas. If anyone feels sick, he need not expect the least attention from the crew; for hogs too are subject to seasickness, and in their case the malady is attended by a splenetic languor and a distaste for life that must be combated at all costs. Forswearing all pity and humanity in order to save the lives of his beloved clients, the captain in person, armed with a whip, plunges into their midst. He is followed by the sailors and cabin-boys, each snatching up whatever lies to hand, whether an iron bar or a rope end, and in a moment the whole herd, which were lying inertly on their sides, are given a fatherly hiding, forced to rise, move around, and counteract by violent exercise the baneful influence of the ship's rolling or pitching.

On our return journey to Barcelona, in the month of March, it was stifling hot, yet we were unable to set foot on deck. Even had we braved the danger of having our legs lopped off by some bad-tempered hog, the captain would never, I am sure, have allowed us to annoy them by our presence. They remained quiet at first; but, about midnight, the pilot noticed that they were sleeping very dejectedly, in the grip, it seemed, of a black depression. So the whip was prescribed, and regularly, every quarter of an hour, we were woken by such terrible cries and shrieks—of pain and rage from the beaten hogs, of inspired encouragement from the captain to his men, and of emulous oaths from the latter—that on several occasions we believed the hogs to be devouring the crew.

GEORGE SAND Winter in Majorca, 1855
Trans. Robert Graves

Of all travellers in Spain, George Borrow made the greatest reputation among his contemporaries. Much of his writing I find slow and ponderous, but there are passages which create the atmosphere of nineteenth-century Spain more powerfully than any others I know.

THE STORM

We had halted and refreshed ourselves and horses at Bembibre, a village of mud and slate, and which possessed little to attract attention: we were now ascending, for the road was over one of the extreme ledges of these frontier hills which I have before so often mentioned; but the aspect of heaven had blackened, clouds were rolling rapidly from the west over the mountains, and a cold wind was moaning dismally. "There is a storm travelling through the air," said a peasant, whom we overtook, mounted on a wretched mule; "and the Asturians had better be on the look-out, for it is speeding in their direction." He had scarce spoken, when a light, so vivid and dazzling that it seemed as if the whole lustre of the fiery element were concentrated in it, broke around us, filling the whole atmosphere, and covering rock, tree, and mountain with a glare not to be described. The mule of the peasant tumbled prostrate, while the horse I rode reared himself perpendicularly, and turning round, dashed down the hill at headlong speed, which for some time it was impossible to check. The lightning was followed by a peal almost as terrible, but distant, for it sounded hollow and deep; the hills, however, caught up its voice, seemingly repeating it from summit to summit, till it was lost in interminable space. Other flashes and peals succeeded, but slight in comparison, and a few drops of rain descended. The body of the tempest seemed to be over another region. "A hundred families are weeping where that bolt fell," said the peasant when I rejoined him, "for its blaze has blinded my mule at six leagues' distance." He was leading the animal by the bridle, as its sight was evidently affected. "Were the friars still in their nest above there," he continued, "I should say that this was their doing, for they are the cause of all the miseries of the land."

I raised my eyes in the direction in which he pointed. Half-way up the mountain, over whose feet we were wending, jutted forth a black frightful crag, which at an immense altitude overhung the road, and seemed to threaten destruction. It resembled one of those ledges of the rocky mountains in the picture of the Deluge, up to which the terrified fugitives have scrambled from the eager pursuit of the savage and tremendous billows, and from whence they gaze down in horror, whilst above them rise still higher and giddier heights, to which they seem unable to climb. Built on the very edge of this crag stood an edifice, seemingly devoted to the purposes of religion, as I could discern the spire of a church rearing itself high over wall and roof. "That is the house of the Virgin of the Rocks," said the peasant, "and it was lately full of friars, but they have been thrust out, and the only inmates now are owls and ravens." I replied, that their life in such a bleak exposed abode could not have been very enviable, as in winter they must have incurred great risk of perishing with cold. "By no means," said he; "they had the best wood for their braseros and chimneys, and the best wine to warm them at their meals, which were not the most sparing." . . .

The sun was setting fast, and eager to reach Villafranca, where I had determined on resting, and which was still distant three leagues and a half, I made no halt at this place. The road was now down a rapid and crooked descent, which terminated in a valley, at the bottom of which was a long and narrow bridge; beneath it rolled a river, descending from a wide pass between two mountains, for the chain was here cleft, probably by some convulsion of nature. I looked up the pass, and on the hills on both sides. Far above, on my right, but standing forth bold and clear, and catching the last rays of the sun, was the Convent of the Precipices, whilst directly over against it, on the farther side of the valley, rose the perpendicular side of the rival hill, which, to a considerable extent intercepting the light, flung its black shadow over the upper end of the pass, involving it in mysterious darkness. Emerging from the centre of this gloom, with thundering sound, dashed a river, white with foam, and bearing along with it huge stones and branches of trees, for it was the wild Sil hurrying to the ocean from its cradle in the heart of the Asturian hills, and probably swollen by the recent rains.

Hours again passed away. It was now night, and we were in the midst of woodlands, feeling our way, for the darkness was so great that I could scarcely see the length of a yard before my horse's head. The animal seemed uneasy, and would frequently stop short, prick up his ears, and utter a low mournful whine. Flashes of sheet lightning frequently illuminated the black sky, and flung a momentary glare over our path. No sound interrupted the stillness of the night, except the croaking of frogs from some pool or morass. I now bethought me that I was in Spain, the chosen land of the two fiends, assassination and plunder, and how easily two tired and unarmed wanderers might become their victims.

We at last cleared the woodlands, and after proceeding a short distance, the horse gave a joyous neigh, and broke into a smart trot. A barking of dogs speedily reached my ears, and we seemed to be approaching some town or village. In effect we were close to Cacabelos, a town about five miles distant from Villafranca.

It was nearly eleven at night, and I reflected that it would be far more expedient to tarry in this place till morning . . . but I reckoned without my host, for at the first posada which I attempted to enter, I was told that we could not be accommodated, and still less our horses, as the stable was full of water. At the second, and there were but two, I was answered from the window by a gruff voice, nearly in the words of the Scripture: "Trouble me not; the door is now shut, and my children are with me in bed; I cannot arise to let you in." Indeed, we had no particular desire to enter, as it appeared a wretched hovel, though the poor horses pawed piteously against the door, and seemed to crave admittance.

We had now no choice but to resume our doleful way to Villafranca, which, we were told, was a short league distant, though it proved a league and a half. We found it no easy matter to quit the town, for we were bewildered amongst its labyrinths, and could not find the outlet. A lad about eighteen was, however, persuaded, by the promise of a peseta, to guide us: whereupon he led us by many turnings to a bridge, which he told us to cross, and to follow the road, which was that to Villafranca; he then, having received his fee, hastened from us.

We followed his directions, not, however, without a suspicion that he might be deceiving us. The night had settled darker down upon us, so that it was impossible to distinguish any object, however nigh. The lightning had become more faint and rare. We heard the rustling of trees, and occasionally the barking of dogs, which last sound, however, soon ceased, and we were in the midst of night and silence. My horse, either from weariness, or the badness of the road, frequently stumbled; whereupon I dismounted, and leading him by the bridle, soon left Antonio far in the rear.

I had proceeded in this manner a considerable way, when a circumstance occurred of a character well suited to the time and place.

I was again amidst trees and bushes, when the horse stopping short, nearly pulled me back. I know not how it was, but fear suddenly came over me, which, though in darkness and in solitude, I had not felt before. I was about to urge the animal forward, when I heard a noise at my right hand, and listened attentively. It seemed to be that of a person or persons forcing their way through branches and brushwood. It soon ceased, and I heard feet on the road. It was the short staggering kind of tread of people carrying a very heavy substance, nearly too much for their strength, and I thought I heard the hurried breathing of men over-fatigued. There was a short pause, during which I conceived they were resting in the middle of the road; then the stamping recommenced, until it reached the other side, when I again heard a similar rustling amidst branches: it continued for some time and died gradually away.

I continued my road, musing on what had just occurred, and forming conjectures as to the cause. The lightning resumed its flashing, and I saw that I was approaching tall black mountains.

This nocturnal journey endured so long that I almost lost all hope of reaching the town, and had closed my eyes in a doze, though I still trudged on mechanically, leading the horse. Suddenly a voice at a slight distance before me roared out, *"Quien vive?"* for I had at last found my way to Villafranca. It proceeded from the sentry in the suburb, one of those singular half soldiers half guerillas, called Miguelets, who are in general employed by the Spanish government to clear the road of robbers. I gave the usual answer *"España"*, and went up to the place where he stood. After a little conversation, I sat down on a stone, awaiting the arrival of Antonio, who was long in making his appearance.

The Bible in Spain, 1843

In the time of George Borrow and Richard Ford there were still no Spanish railways, and, it seemed, not likely to be.

178

OF MULETEERS AND RAILWAYS

The first cholera that visits Spain will be set down as a passenger per rail by the dispossessed muleteer, who now performs the functions of steam and rail. He constitutes one of the most numerous and finest classes in Spain, and is the legitimate channel of the semi-Oriental caravan system. He will never permit the bread to be taken out of his mouth by this Lutheran locomotive; deprived of means of earning his livelihood, he, like the smuggler, will take to the road in another line, and both will become either robbers or patriots. Many, long, and lonely are the leagues which separate town from town in the wide deserts of thinly-peopled Spain, nor will any preventive service be sufficient to guard the rail against the *guerilla* warfare that may then be waged. A handful of opponents in any cistus-overgrown waste, may at any time, in five minutes, break up the road, stop the train, stick the stoker, and burn the engines in their own fire, particularly smashing the luggage-train.

RICHARD FORD *Gatherings from Spain*

But the railways came.

BY LADIES' COUPÉ

Always travel in your best clothes, and with half-a-dozen trunks at least. Luggage and good clothes take the place of a train of servants. Luggage and good clothes ensure you good places, general civility, and an infinity of minor comforts. . . .

It is all very well for savages to travel without luggage— the Japanese Grandees don't even carry pocket-handkerchiefs about with them, but if any one wants to travel pleasantly and profitably, let him carry a well stored portmanteau. Surely in no country but patient Spain would two ladies have been allowed to fill the first-class compartment of a railway carriage in the way we did. Under the seats, on the seats, above the seats, were piled an infinite variety of packages, a box of medicines, a folding india-rubber bath, a basket of provisions (a precaution never to be neglected), two or three parcels of books, two or three bundles of rugs, a leather bag of sketching materials, sketching blocks of various sizes, a silk bag of needles and threads; lastly, an odd bag, containing note-books, opera glasses, passports, a tea-pot, a water bottle, an etna, an air-cushion, slippers, and sundries without number.

And everything was so useful in its turn. In that long slow railway journey through Spain, we were, as I have said, always alone. We breakfasted, we dined, we wrote letters and diaries, we read all our books from beginning to end, and we mended our clothes, we made sketches, we made tea, we might have refreshed ourselves with a cold bath, but for want of water. Not a bit of our precious luggage could we have spared.

MATILDA BETHAM EDWARDS
Through Spain to the Sahara

Later came the buses, at first with those seats on their roofs which never appear to have been found acceptable in other countries and which seem to lead inevitably to the passing of wine bottles from hand to hand, making the dullest journey into a party. I remember near Tarragona, in slightly self-conscious imitation of Hemingway, getting quite drunk on a bus roof and, when it wouldn't stop at the aqueduct I wanted to see, trying to jump off the back ladder. Walter Starkie remembers travelling inside buses.

BY BUS

Then women were not so accustomed to bus travelling as they are today, and I have vivid memories of their behaviour. No sooner did the crowded vehicle begin to skid round corners on its upward or downward corkscrew course than with one accord they were violently sick and we became a nightmare bus with pale, ghostly women craning their necks out of the windows on both sides like geese in a crate being driven to market. I used in those days, as a prudent precaution, invariably to give up my window seat to any lady travelling in my proximity, so that she might lean out to her heart's content.

The Road to Santiago

Perhaps it is a pity that we don't still have to visit Spain by mule or donkey, waggon or diligence.

TODAY

A day later we came to Madrid, and here we stayed at the Savoy, a large, comfortable hotel with open-air dining-terrace on the roof, dance-floor and also—it was true after all—a swimming-pool. Again there was little cause for complaint. Mr Whinny, however, found something that displeased him: the entrance to the hotel, he said, was not pretentious enough for one that was rated first class: so did Mr Snort who declared that in the restaurant—it was too cold in Madrid in May to dine on the open-air terrace—he could not get a hot plate. He pronounced it "hot plight" as though it were a difficult situation he was after. I was to inform the agency, he told me, when I next made a report, that all over Spain the "plights" had been cold; and couldn't they do something about it. His next grouse was directed at me. I had failed to tell him that he ought to visit the Royal Palace, which had not been included in our official sightseeing of Madrid. He had gone to it on someone else's advice and found that it was better than anything he had yet seen: better even than Fontainebleau had been: better even than Versailles could possibly be.

After two days in Madrid we moved on to Burgos and arrived in that small city (which boasts the second most beautiful Gothic cathedral in Spain) in time for lunch.

In Burgos the quality of hotel had to go down considerably, and again I had trouble over bathrooms. When the allocation of rooms was finished, two of the South Africans assailed me in a fury, because they had not been given private bathrooms whereas a number of other people had. I explained that two of the party had come to me as we were nearing Burgos (expecting a drop in the standard of hotel) and asked me to arrange private bathrooms for them for which they would willingly pay the additional cost. That did not matter, said the woman. It had been pointed out to them before they left that the tour included bathrooms at all those hotels where there were any. At this one there was a bathroom to every second room: they had learnt that from the receptionist; and since they had not been given one, the facts had been misrepresented. "Don't argue with him," she concluded, turning to her husband impatiently. "We will take it up with the agency." They then went back to the reception and squandered their entire allowance of pocket-money for the day on paying for a private bathroom.

Nor were they the only ones to be annoyed. The ill-humoured American was the next to complain. He had not been given a bathroom either, he said. I explained all over again that at that particular hotel no bathrooms had been promised. The American declared that any tour in which bathrooms were not promised at every stop was no tour at all; and with that he strode off to his bedroom only to reappear a few minutes later cursing more than ever. His room, he had found, had not yet been made up. I asked the reception to have it prepared immediately. The American said that that kinda thing made him lose confidence, and he only hoped the sheets wouldn't be wet. One of the Australian women had told him that the sheets had been wet in both Granada and Alicante and that on that account she had caught a cold.

WILLIAM HONEY *Travel Courier in Spain,* 1960

ACKNOWLEDGEMENTS

Grateful acknowledgement is due to the following authors, agents and publishers for permission to include copyright material:

V. S. Pritchett and Chatto & Windus Ltd for passages from *The Spanish Temper* (pages 5-7, 14-15, 23-25, 110, 123-124 and 128); Mrs Ilsa Barea for a passage from her translation of Arturo Barea, *The Track*, published by Faber & Faber Ltd (pages 7-8); Jarrolds Publishers (London) Ltd for a passage from *Ponies and Women* by Col. T. P. Melvill (page 10); George Weidenfeld & Nicolson Ltd for a passage from *The People of the Sierra* by J. A. Pitt- Rivers (pages 10-11) and a passage from *Great Houses of Europe* by Hugh Thomas (pages 36-38); Penguin Books Ltd for passages from J. M. Cohen's translation of *Don Quixote* (pages 12-13 and 53-54); Routledge & Kegan Paul Ltd for a passage from André Malraux's *L'Espoir*, trans. S. Gilbert and A. Macdonald (pages 73-75); John Haycraft and Hamish Hamilton Ltd for passages from *Babel in Spain* (pages 13-14, 57, 99, 101-104, 119 and 151); Sacheverell Sitwell with B. T. Batsford Ltd for passages from *Spain* (pages 19-20 and 29-30)—and with Gerald Duckworth & Co. Ltd for a passage from *Spanish Baroque Art* (page 29); John Calder (Publishers) Ltd for J. R. Longland's translation "Axa, Fátima and Marién" (page 20) and a passage from *El Burlador de Sevilla* by Tirso de Molina, trans. Harry Kemp (pages 107-109) included in *An Anthology of Spanish Literature*, compiled by Seymour and Pasmantier, 1958 (42s); *Navy Records Society* for passages from *The Tangier Papers of Samuel Pepys*, ed. Edwin Chappell (pages 21 and 163); the Roy Campbell Estate with The Bodley Head Ltd for two poems from Roy Campbell's *Collected Poems* (pages 120-121 and 150)—with Faber & Faber Ltd for two poems from *Talking Bronco* (pages 88-89 and 105)—and with Bowes & Bowes Publishers Ltd for two passages from *Lorca* (pages 138 and 145); Chatto & Windus Ltd for passages from *The Great Teresa* by Elizabeth Hamilton (pages 25 and 26-27) and from *Elizabeth and Essex* by Lytton Strachey (pages 85-86 and 86-87); Gertrude Bone and Macmillan & Co. Ltd for passages from *Days In Old Spain* (pages 27-28 and 95-97); Methuen & Co. Ltd for passages from *A Stranger in Spain* by H. V. Morton (pages 33-34, 38-39 and 55-56); Hamish Hamilton Ltd for passages from *Fabled Shore* by Rose Macaulay

(pages 39–41 and 173–174) and from *South From Granada* by
Gerald Brenan (pages 45–48, 55, 151–153, 161 and 162);
Anthony Carson and Methuen & Co. Ltd for passages from
Looking For a Bandit (pages 41–44 and 135–137); Cassell & Co.
Ltd for passages from *Love and the Spanish* by Nina Epton
(pages 45, 56 and 57); University Press Cambridge for a
passage from *The Literature of the Spanish People* (page 105)
by Gerald Brenan; Luzac & Co. Ltd for a passage from A. J.
Arberry's translation of Ibn Hazm, *The Ring of the Dove* (page
53); Joyce Weiner Associates and Herbert Jenkins Ltd
for a passage from *Mantillas And Me* by Barbara Borbolla
(pages 57–58); The Society of Authors (literary representative
of the Havelock Ellis Estate) for a passage from *Soul of Spain*
by Havelock Ellis, published by Constable & Co. Ltd (page
59); Miss D. E. Collins for an extract from "Lepanto" by
G. K. Chesterton (pages 59–61); John Johnson, Author's
Agent, for a passage from *Horses of the Conquest* by R. B.
Cunningham-Graham, published by William Heinemann Ltd
(pages 69–70); Faber & Faber Ltd for a passage from "Spain"
by W. H. Auden (page 73) and passages from *Sherry* by Julian
Jeffs (pages 168 and 169); Martin Secker & Warburg Ltd for
passages from *Homage to Catalonia* by George Orwell (pages
75–77, 77 and 77–78) and a passage from J. E. Flecker's translation "Lord Arnaldos" (pages 112–113); Hutchinson & Co.
(Publishers) Ltd for a passage from *The Epic of the Alcazar* by
Geoffrey Moss (pages 79–80); Kate O'Brien and William Heinemann Ltd for a passage from *Farewell Spain* (pages 81–82);
The Unicorn Press (London) Ltd for passages from *Queens
of Old Spain* by Martin Hume (pages 82–83 and 154)
and from *Spain, Her Life And Arts* by Royall Tyler (pages 110,
155–156), both published by Grant Richards; Longmans, Green
& Co. Ltd for passages from *The Spanish Journal of Elizabeth
Lady Holland*, ed. the Earl of Ilchester (pages 154–155 and 163),
and a passage from *English Seamen of the Sixteenth Century* by
J. A. Froude (page 87); Peter Owen Ltd for passages from
A. E. Murch's translation of Alexandre Dumas, *Paris To Cadiz*
(pages 90, 140–141, 153 and 172); Violet Alford for
passages from her *Pyrenean Festivals*, published by Chatto &
Windus Ltd (pages 91 and 91–93); the Literary Executor of
George Santayana and Constable & Co. Ltd for a passage from
Persons and Places (pages 94–95); Jonathan Cape Ltd for
passages from *The Sun Also Rises* (pages 98 and 143–144)
and a passage from *Death in the Afternoon* (pages 141–143) by
Ernest Hemingway; John Murray (Publishers) Ltd for passages
from *The Road to Santiago* (pages 98–99 and 180) and
Spanish Raggle-Taggle (pages 133–134) by Walter Starkie; Don
Salvador de Madariaga for a passage from his *Essays With A*

Purpose, published by Hollis & Carter Ltd (pages 105–107); The New English Library Ltd for a passage from J. M. Cohen's translation *Blind Man's Boy* (pages 111–112); The Society of Authors and Dr John Masefield, O.M., for Dr Masefield's translation of "Rima LXXVIII" by Gustavo Adolfo Bécquer (pages 115–117); Alfred A. Knopf Inc. for passages from C. A. Phillips' translation of *Un Voyage En Espagne* by Théophile Gautier (pages 121–122 and 170); Hurst & Blackett Ltd for passages from *Through Spain to the Sahara* by Matilda Betham Edwards (pages 129–130 and 179–180); Gerald Duckworth & Co. Ltd for the poem "Tarantella" by Hilaire Belloc (pages 130–131); Peter Davies Ltd for a passage from *The Life and Death of a Spanish Town* by Elliot Paul (pages 131–132); Macmillan & Co. Ltd for a passage from *Notes on a Cellar-Book* by George Saintsbury (page 168) and a passage from *The Chronicles of Froissart*, trans. Lord Berners, ed. G. C. Macaulay (pages 70–72); Leslie Charteris for passages from his translation of Juan Belmonte, *Killer of Bulls* (pages 146–148 and 148–150); Putnam & Co. Ltd for a passage from *Sherry* by Rupert Croft-Cooke (pages 165–166); International Authors N.V. and Cassell & Co. Ltd for a passage from Robert Graves' translation of George Sand, *Winter in Majorca* (pages 174–175); William Honey and International Literary Management for a passage from *Travel Courier in Spain*, published by Robert Hale Ltd (pages 180–181).

Acknowledgement is also due to the following photographers and agencies for permission to reproduce photographs:

Camera Press Ltd (facing pages 48, 88, 105, 113, and 152); J. Allan Cash, FIBP, FRPS (between 48 and 49 (The Alcazar), facing pages 49, 80, 104, 112, 137, 153); Robert Capa-Magnum and the John Hillelson Agency (facing page 72); Rosa Harvan—Black Star Pictures (facing page 89); and Trauttmansdorff—Black Star Pictures (facing page 121).

The front endpaper photograph of bull training near Madrid is by Arthur Brilliant, and is reproduced by permission of Camera Press Ltd; the back endpaper photograph of Avila is reproduced by courtesy of the Spanish National Tourist Office.